Spring 2014

Bing Wang/A. Eugene Kohn

Global Leadership in Real Estate and Design

Global Leadership in Real Estate and Design

Within the global constellation of increasingly connected urban centers, shifts in cultural preferences, design thinking, and spatial signification often reflect parallel transitions in capital forces and economic realities, locally and across the globe. The premise of the Global Leadership in Real Estate and Design course at the Harvard University Graduate School of Design lies in the belief that globalization inexorably imposes unprecedented forces and tensions that directly impact the formation and production of the urban built environment.

The pedagogical focus of this course is twofold: to establish an intellectual framework for students to understand and embrace the interrelationship between real estate and design so that creativity and design thinking become a value-adding and differentiating component in real estate thought leadership and development; and to encourage students to rethink, anticipate, and reinvent practice paradigms in an academic setting that respond to exigent and transformative environmental, market, and cultural changes, while fully leveraging an active, semester-long engagement with contemporaneous but ever-shifting global urban contexts.

Instructors
Bing Wang, A. Eugene Kohn

Students
Fabiana Alvear, Patrick Boateng II, Alessandro Boccacci, Matthew Ciccotti, Zhewen Dai, Stefan Di Leo, Luis Gil, Dylan Lazovik, Chen Ling, Aaron Locke, Terry Lu, Jason McAlees, Christine Min, Frankie Refuerzo, Emmanuel Torres, Kyle Trulen, Brian Vargo, Han Wang, Heng Zhang, Ying Zhang

Research Assistants
Yong K. Kim, Yunjie Li, Wei Lin, Zhuangzhuang Song, Man Su

Review Critics
Sven Andersen, Donald Chiofaro, Donald Conover, Robert Greenwood, Bing Hu, Thomas Hussey, Blair Kamin, Thomas Kearns, Matthew Lynch, Matthias Luecker, Theodore Oatis, Thomas Schneider, Raymond Torto, Frank Wuest

Preface
9 Bing Wang

14 Innovative Juncture:
Real Estate and Design
Bing Wang

23 Leadership in Design
A. Eugene Kohn

26 Design Formulates the Next
Wave in the Real Estate Industry
Sven Andersen and Thomas Schneider

29 Place and Profit: Assessing the
Plans of Global Leadership in
Real Estate and Design
Blair Kamin

**Project I:
Mediating Between Static and
Fluid Urban Systems
Guangzhou, China**

36 Thoughts and Reflections:
Developing Leadership in Real
Estate and Design
Brian Vargo

40 Articulating the Programmed
Ecosystem: The Haizhu Gardens
Patrick Boateng II, Matthew Ciccotti,
and Brian Vargo

48 Urban Stratification:
Augmented Eminence
Stefan Di Leo, Aaron Locke,
and Terry Lu

60 Burgeoning Iconic-ism in
Vernacular Urban Conditions
Aaron Locke

62 Composing the Productive
Eco-Lifestyle
Zhewen Dai, Jason McAlees, and
Frankie Refuerzo

66 Art River:
Typological Archipelago
Luis Gil, Christine Min, and
Han Wang

**Project II:
Urbanistic Convergence
Boston, MA USA**

80 Vertical Urbanism: The Pivot
Fabiana Alvear and Kyle Trulen

90 Projecting Context
Thomas Hussey

94 Connection
Thomas Kearns

98 Monumental Interlace
Chen Ling, Emmanuel Torres, and
Heng Zhang

106 Bridging Thresholds:
Interconnecting the
Boston Waterfront
Alessandro Boccacci, Dylan Lazovik,
and Ying Zhang

120 Contributors

Preface

In the complex and intricate realm of the built environment, thoughtful and deliberate interaction between the once partitioned real estate and design fields is positively influencing the ultimate quality, form, scale, and economic sustainability of the global urbanism. Indeed, the increasingly multidimensional nature of real estate development raises questions about whether students and professionals trained separately in traditional real estate or design studies will be well prepared to embrace multifaceted risks and to successfully lead as practitioners or thought leaders.

The pedagogical belief of the Global Leadership in Real Estate and Design course, not unlike that of the Master in Design Studies Real Estate program at the Harvard University Graduate School of Design, is that there must be convergence and integration in the teaching and study of real estate and design, especially through underlying research, design studios (the equivalent of field studies) methodology and production processes, cross-functional case studies, and exploration via thematic and multifaceted analyses (whether based on design or a spreadsheet). This pedagogical approach has not been addressed adequately within the existing professional and academic environment or in the literature, which have continued to uphold the convenient segregation of these vertical, one-dimensional domains rather than championing an integrated interdisciplinary or holistic approach. Thus the GSD Global Leadership course aims to expand the study of the intersection between real estate and design to a broader spectrum of interpretation. We seek to challenge the barriers to the field, and question the design and real estate disciplines' current positions, conventional approaches, scope, and values.

Taught by myself and Gene Kohn, the Global Leadership course for Spring 2014 enrolled 22 students with a wide range of academic backgrounds, professional orientations, and skill sets—real estate, economics, finance, urban design, planning, architecture, and landscape architecture. Two vastly dissimilar projects and site settings were intentionally selected for the course: one a waterfront redevelopment in Boston and the other along the southern axis of a new business district in Guangzhou, China. Divided into groups of two or three, the students were assigned by lottery to work on one of these two projects throughout the semester. Although the scale, location, and programs were different for the two sites, students were guided with parallel dialogues and orientation sessions to confront the relationships between real estate and design, and to conflate the external realities of macroeconomic trends, cultural shifts, regulatory constraints, and real estate capital market requirements into well-informed design strategies and development proposals. This process helped to inspire a greater sensitivity toward purpose, context, external demands, and the urban built environment, and a striving to enhance the intellectual and physical dynamism between real estate and design.

Throughout the semester, students had in-person opportunities to confront, engage, and negotiate the competing interests of the different stakeholders involved in the two projects. They were able to devise and recalibrate their decisions for development strategies and for design proposals to be either more self-servingly spatial than socially friendly, more physically imposing than politically correct, more financially rewarding than aesthetically appealing, or vice versa, and with many more permutations and choices. The goal was to demonstrate that the most appropriate design thinking is not often utopian but an aggregation and synthesis anchored by a balance of cultural, social, and market realism.

Moreover, the course participants came to appreciate that the goal was no longer to design and construct an idealized, stand-alone physical structure, but, instead, rather to create a negotiated and optimized physical space and societal place by navigating the dichotomies often neglected in conventional design education: public interest vs. private benefits, financial gain vs. aesthetic preference, etc. Just as Peggy Deamer asserted, "the history of architecture is the history of capital," urban design and architecture in the Global Leadership in Real Estate and Design course is are integrated with this understanding of capital. Student teams allocate different weights to economics and design in their final proposals. More creative design solutions and development schemes do not necessarily lead to less successful economic performance. This GSD course presents a framework for situating the two aspects within the context of a complex urban development in the global arena, and explores the potential of alternative working methods combining that combined strategies for design, development, and implementation, with an interdisciplinary articulation.

I am grateful to Dean Mohsen Mostafavi for his vision in expanding the connections between the realms of design and real estate, and for his belief in the richness of cross-disciplinary pursuits at the GSD. I would also like to thank Michael Hays, Pat Roberts, Rahul Mehrotra, Iñaki Ábalos, Peter Rowe, Rick Peiser, and Gene Kohn for their unwavering support for of pedagogical experimentation in the Global Leadership in Real Estate and Design course and beyond. Furthermore, I am also grateful to the enrolled students for their passion, curiosity, and open-mindedness in exploring design and real estate through different lenses, and as well as for their willingness to journey beyond the conventional boundaries of their disciplines to collaborate, challenge, and appreciate each other's knowledge realms.

—Bing Wang, March 2015

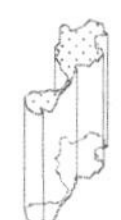

1795 DENSITY
5,689 population/sqkm

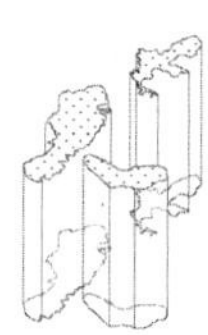

1836 DENSITY
7,097 population/sqkm

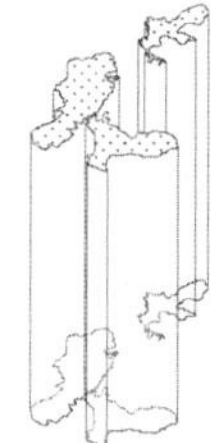

1855 DENSITY
14,024 population/sqkm

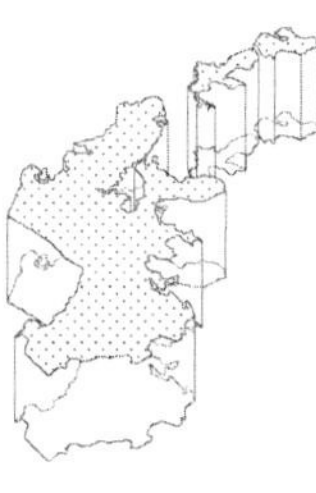

1869 DENSITY
4,335 population/sqkm

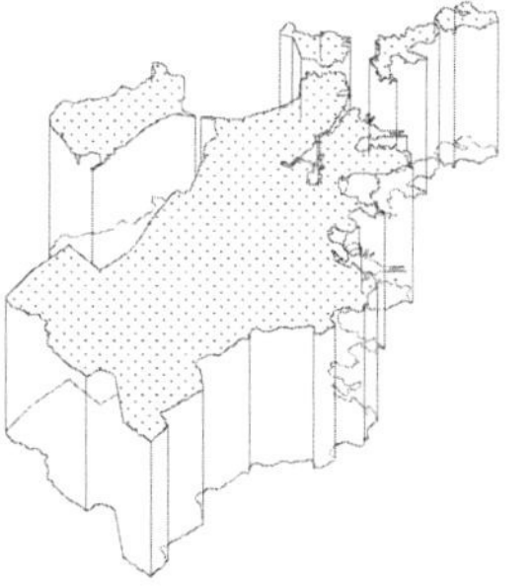

1912 DENSITY
6,916 population/sqkm

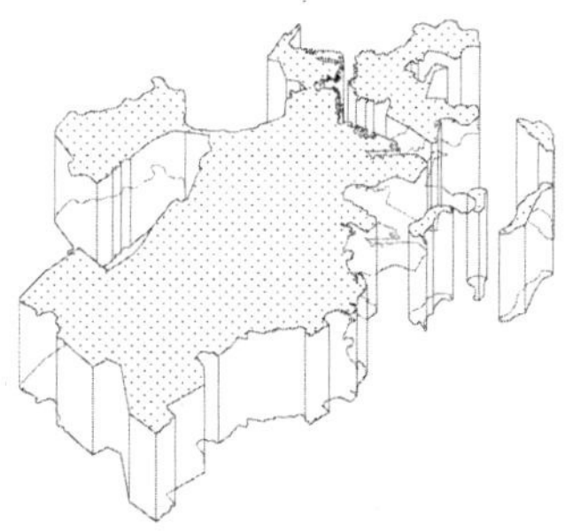

2012 DENSITY
5,112 population/sqkm

The historical evolution of Boston's city boundary, population growth, and resulting urban density. Boston's urbanization has been driven by reconfiguration of geographical limits and boundaries through the historical practice of land reclamation. Boston data provided by http://physics.bu.edu/~redner/projects/population/cities/boston.html and U.S. Census Bureau.

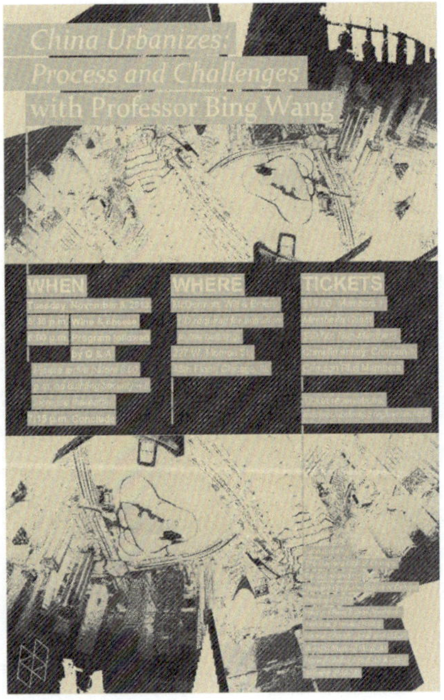

MDes Real Estate and the Built Environment event posters of 2013–2014 school semesters at the Harvard University Graduate School of Design. The pedagogical framework of converging real estate and design practices include multifaceted processes, traversing both academic and professional realms through projective research, development proposals, and interactive platforms to broaden the contemporary paradigms of academic and professional practices.

GLOBAL LEADERSHIP IN REAL ESTATE + DESIGN LECTURE SERIES
XIN ZHANG
CEO SOHO CHINA
THURSDAY, OCTOBER 17, 2013
3:00 – 4:00 PM
PIPER AUDITORIUM
48 QUINCY STREET
CAMBRIDGE, MA 02138
WWW.GSD.HARVARD.EDU
As the largest commercial real estate developer in China, SOHO China plays a leading role in China's urbanization. Under Xin Zhang's leadership, SOHO China has continually translated the innovative designs of internationally acclaimed architects ZAHA HADID, KENGO KUMA, DAVID ADJAYE, GARY CHANG, ANTONIA OCHOA, KPF, UNSTUDIO, ORDER OF FILAIL PHASE, QINGYUN MA, RIKEN YAMAMOTO, COLIN SEAH, SHIGERU BAN, ROCCO YIM, PETER DAVIDSON, AND GMP, into iconic real estate - redefining the modern architectural landscape of Beijing and Shanghai.
Repeatedly listed by Forbes as one of the "World's 100 Most Powerful Women," Xin Zhang was the first non-architect to receive an award at the Venice Biennale for her commissioning of the "Commune by the Great Wall", a collection of contemporary architecture designed by twelve Asian architects.
Harvard University
Graduate School of Design

Tang Jun
President & Executive Director
Beijing Capital Land
Monday, November 4, 2013
1pm to 4pm
Gund Hall, Portico 121
48 Quincy St. Cambridge, MA 02138
MDes REAL ESTATE
GLOBAL LEADERSHIP IN REAL ESTATE + DESIGN LECTURE SERIES
Harvard University
Graduate School of Design

Harvard University
Graduate School of Design
INTERDISCIPLINARY REAL ESTATE EDUCATION AT HARVARD
5:30pm to 7:00pm
Wednesday, September 17, 2014
Gund Hall, Portico 121
48 Quincy Street, Cambridge, MA 02138
• What makes real estate education unique at the Harvard Graduate School of Design?
• How does the MDes Real Estate program prepare students to become global thought leaders in real estate?
• What is the nature of interdisciplinary study in real estate?
Listen to perspectives on these questions and more from GSD professors Bing Wang, Richard Peiser, Raymond Torto, and Frank Apeseche.

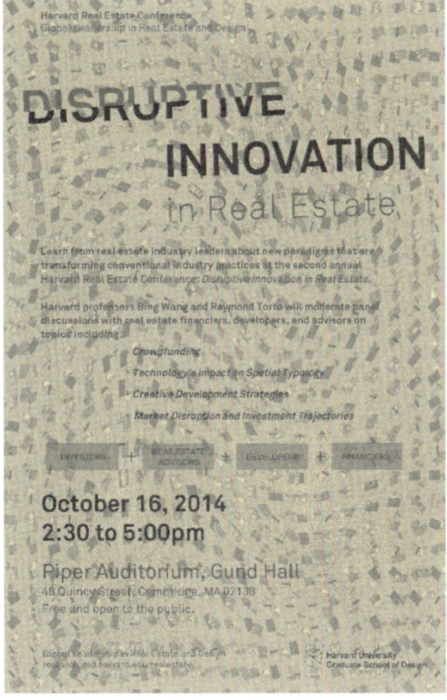
Harvard Real Estate Conference
DISRUPTIVE INNOVATION in Real Estate
Learn from real estate industry leaders about new paradigms that are transforming conventional industry practices at the second annual Harvard Real Estate Conference: Disruptive Innovation in Real Estate.
Harvard professors Bing Wang and Raymond Torto will moderate panel discussions with real estate financiers, developers, and advisors on topics including:
Crowdfunding
Technology's impact on Spatial Typology
Creative Development Strategies
Market Disruption and Investment Trajectories
October 16, 2014
2:30 to 5:00pm
Piper Auditorium, Gund Hall
Free and open to the public.
Harvard University
Graduate School of Design

Innovative Juncture: Real Estate and Design

Bing Wang

Design and real estate are inherently intertwined, but this linkage is not easy to dissect or analyze without encountering the obvious danger of oversimplification.

Design is often closely associated with an emphasis on form and aesthetics, while real estate has a focus on implementation and process. The interaction between these two fields inevitably creates new perspectives and methods, and sometimes, also, possible hybrids that bring valuable additions to the existing repertoire of design and development vocabularies, prompting new ways of thinking as we construct a workable, even innovative, urbanism for the future.

Despite the differences in focus, real estate and design share certain intrinsic commonalities. Both contribute powerfully to building physical environments that reflect vision and imagination. Both offer a unique array of knowledge, operational skills, and intelligence that must be synthesized to produce a suitable outcome or product, whether a set of drawings or a fully finished building. In design, for example, one needs to deal with the structural, environmental, and acoustical aspects among others, of a building, landscape, or city, while in real estate development one must cope with design, financing, construction, environmental concerns, and much more.

As the world becomes increasingly interconnected, emerging social, technological, and economic circumstances will constantly demand that the skills and strategies applied in both design and real estate interact and communicate to effectively counter market-driven sprawl and the socially destructive forces of poorly considered urbanization. Bridging the two fields, however, will not be an easy task. In this context, the Global Leadership in Real Estate and Design course can serve as a valuable stimulus for further academic interest and creative exploration by revisiting and reinterpreting the foundations and approaches of the two disciplines. It can also be a call to examine alternative modes of inquiry of an interdisciplinary pedagogy that does not diminish the originality and autonomy of each discipline.

The Course

Today's world has witnessed an increasingly complex built environment that needs to address the combination of the high speed of change, technological invention, rapid globalization, and an embedded multitude of cultural meanings. Thus teaching the combination of real estate and design in a classroom setting becomes critical and exciting. Reinforcing design thinking and creativity within complex urban projects must be aimed for, not just to be artistic and speculative, but also to be strategic. Design and development solutions need to be multilayered yet fully compatible with the complex implementation processes of today's and tomorrow's built environment. Addressing them requires a full knowledge of real estate and a constant negotiation between design and development.

The Global Leadership course attests to this constant and evolving negotiation between form and capital operations, between aesthetics and project economics. It unapologetically exposes complexity and introduces an element

Top: Unknown artist, *View of Canton* (Guangzhou, China), ca. 1800. Courtesy, Peabody Essex Museum.

Bottom: J. Carwitham, *A South-East View of the City of Boston in North America*. Courtesy, Yale Center for British Art.

of realism in addressing a project's process in an academic setting. In this context, form becomes an expression of the complexity and subtlety that is reflected in the process, and the result of constant negotiation among a variety of forces—cultural, aesthetic, economic, social, and political. This form-producing procedure can provide a methodological framework for expanding the dialogue among multi-sector stakeholders.

Applying this framework during the semester, each student team defines its own method of negotiation and formulation of programs, and, with the guidance of the professors, frames the specified constraints that, along with creativity, are crucial to guiding the learning process. To create design proposals and development strategies that respect and respond to the particularities of sites, students quickly realize the importance of comprehensive due diligence: dissecting data and analyzing macro-level social, political, and economic information; and understanding how data and trends can interact in a visual design process. Thus cultural and social sensitivity informs economic market realism to create imaginative yet grounded proposals. These speculative designs become the foundation of students' intellectual inquiries and expanded thought processes.

Throughout the course, students test the economic viability of each proposal, via analysis of finances and strategies for implementation, to define the context of each project within an urban built environment. This rigorous approach reinforces the centrality of design creativity and innovation when confronting both locational and temporal challenges. Students are required to have a design vision, but concurrently embrace an economic point of view, addressing the financial means as well as the spatial strategies for their work. Each design vision is implemented through economic strategies, and the economic vision is facilitated by the design solution.

Through the students' hands-on experience, creative propositions, risk-taking judgment training, and the exercise of leadership in real estate and design projects in the real world, this course integrates domestic and international field studies, lectures, and class discussions. It encourages students to rethink, anticipate, and reinvent practice paradigms in both the real estate and the design fields, and respond to a projected transformative context of market, economic, and cultural changes. The course also offers a highly interactive, semester-long engagement with accomplished real estate and design leaders.

This course is an experiment in the interdisciplinary teaching of design and real estate; the complexities of that relationship and the interconnection between the subjective, artistic component of design and objectivity in measuring the economic and financial performance of a development proposal call for further in-depth investigation and new modes of inquiry.

The Sites

As in a typical design studio, the physical site acts in some respects as a tabula rasa for creativity and imagination, as students apply their knowledge and skills to achieve the course's pedagogical goals. Yet each site also comes with predefined narratives within a multidimensional context, presenting a case study awaiting optimized solutions, similar to the teaching method often utilized in business schools. Students examine the interrelationships between real estate and design, and their underlying production processes, through a combination of rational market research, analysis of economic shifts, investigation of aesthetic form design and the critique of its performance, and study of the deal structure of private and public joint ventures. The various components of the site converge into a vivid narrative of a final proposal that reflects individual creativity and intelligence.

The importance of site selection speaks to the rationale of the course pedagogy. The sites are located in urban areas and could potentially be developed for a variety of uses of modern urban life: living, playing, and working, among others. The sites also need to be suitable for providing students with an understanding of the dynamics and complexities of real contemporary urban environments, based on their contextual physical, economic, and political interconnections.

Each year two sites are selected and assigned to students through a lottery system; one is located in the United States and the other is in an international location. In 2014, the two sites were in Boston and Guangzhou; in 2015, they are in midtown Manhattan and near the city center of Berlin, Germany. The careful selection of these sites, and the structure of having students work on two sites within a single course, are intended to construct a parallel dialogue about varied scales, programmatic formulations, visual compositions, and typological variations. Thoroughly exploring the two sites raises students' awareness of specific market conditions and increases their sensitivity to cultural nuances relevant to the process of generating creative solutions.

Both selected projects for 2014 were redevelopment cases located on the waterfront. The Boston project focused on how to transform a car-oriented, modernistic urban environment into a vibrant post-industrial urban setting

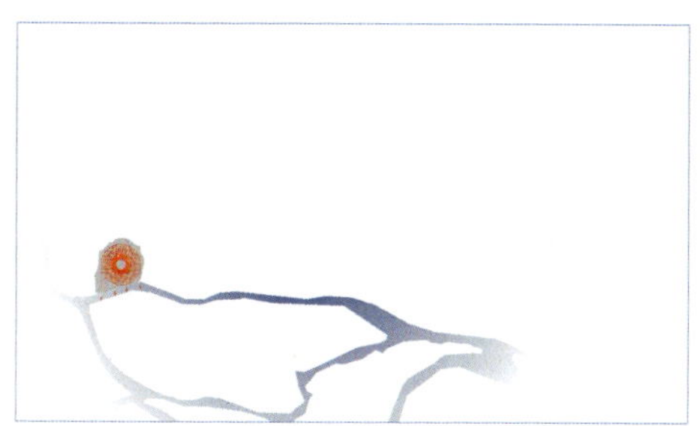

1900 | PORT CITY

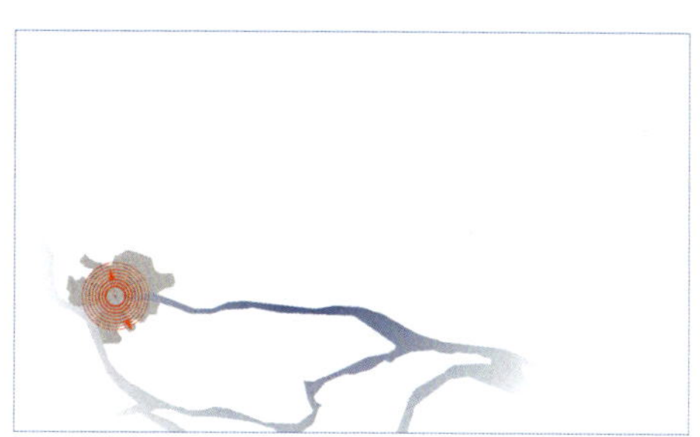

1923 | PORT EXPANSION

1954 | INDUSTRIAL EXPANSION

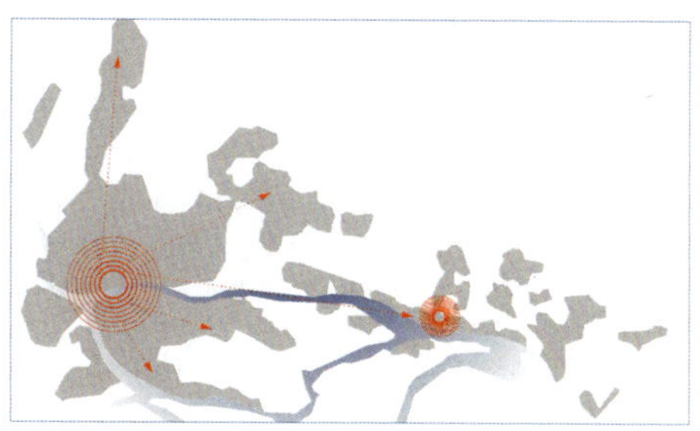

1979 | INDUSTRIAL URBANIZATION

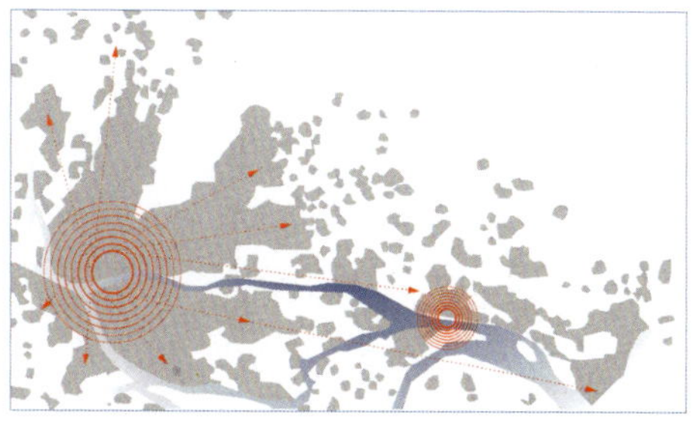

1992 | MODERNIZATION & URBAN SPRAWL

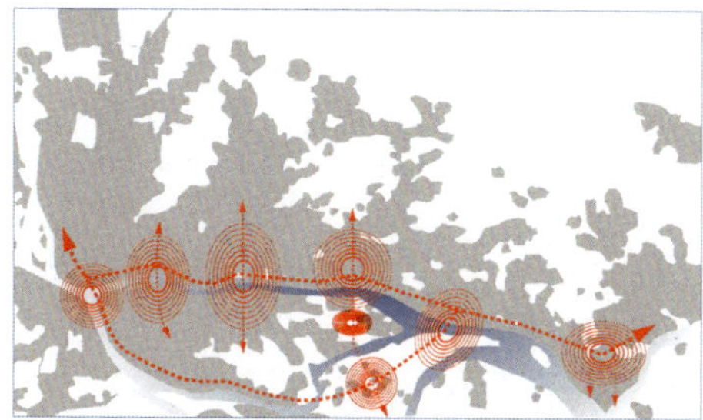

1998 - PRESENT | CONURBANIZATION & POLYCENTRIC CENTRALIZATION

Guangzhou's urban growth is influenced and limited by geographical features such as the dynamic waterfront to the south and static mountains to the north. The current urban master plan focuses on development along the north–south axis, strengthening the city's connection to the urban waterfront.

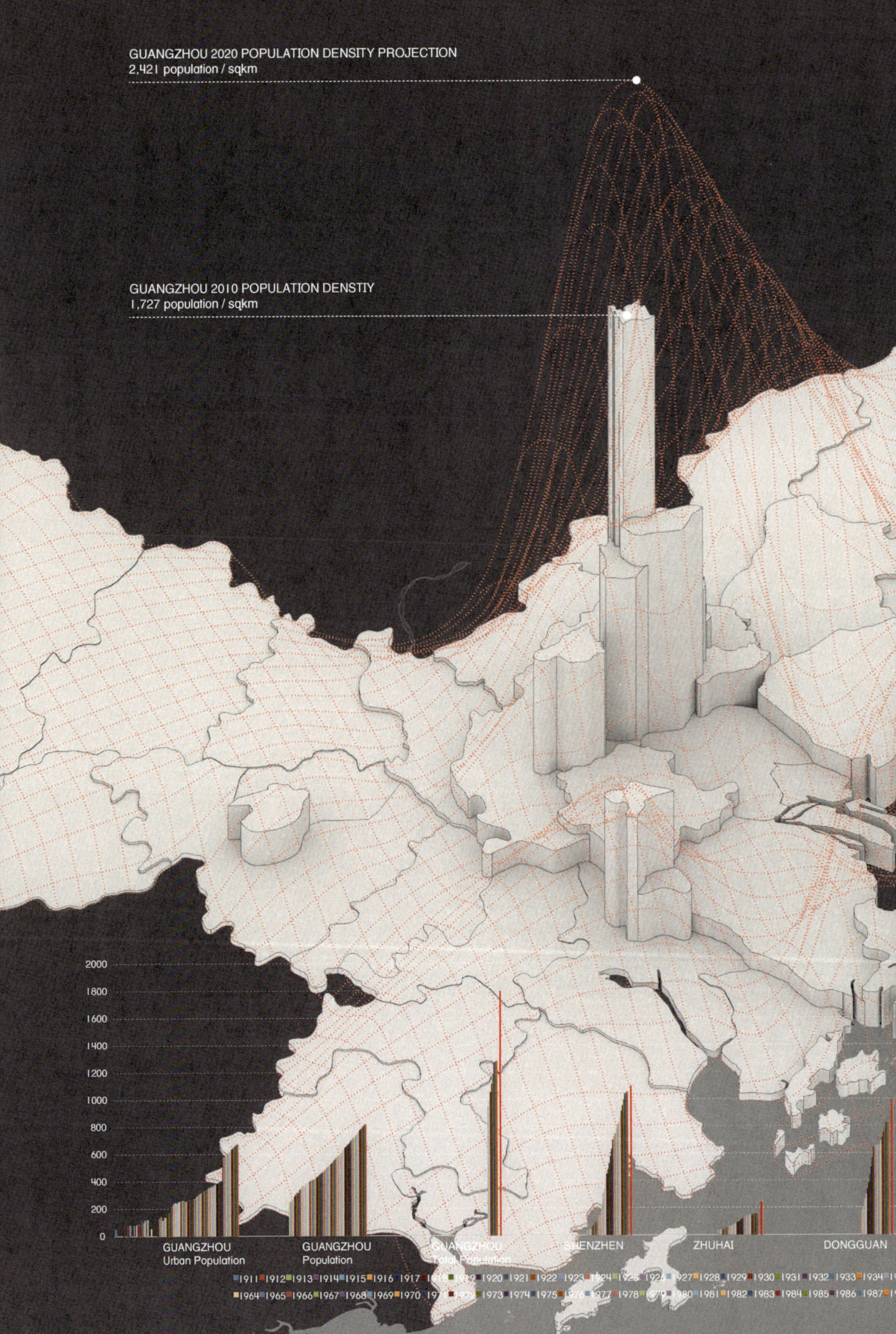
GUANGZHOU 2020 POPULATION DENSITY PROJECTION
2,421 population / sqkm
GUANGZHOU 2010 POPULATION DENSTIY
1,727 population / sqkm
2000
1800
1600
1400
1200
1000
800
600
400
200
0
GUANGZHOU
Urban Population
GUANGZHOU
Population
GUANGZHOU
Total Population
SHENZHEN
ZHUHAI
DONGGUAN
1911 1912 1913 1914 1915 1916 1917 1920 1921 1922 1923 1927 1928 1929 1930 1931 1932 1933 1934
1964 1965 1966 1967 1968 1969 1970 1973 1974 1975 1977 1978 1980 1981 1982 1983 1984 1985 1986 1987

Projecting Density in Urban Agglomeration

HONG KONG 2020 POPULATION DENSITY PROJECTION
7,091 population / sqkm

HONG KONG 2010 POPULATION DENSTIY
6,539 population / sqkm

The increased density caused by rapid economic growth and urbanization in the Pearl River Delta region raises demand for residential units and low-density developments. In contrast to the existing urbanization trends, the low-density developments can offer a desirable and unique product in the future residential market.

Data and GIS source:
World Bank Group DataBank
Harvard University China Historical GIS
Bureau of Statistics and Urban Planning Bureau of Municipalities

ZHONGSHAN JIANGMEN ZHAOQIN HUIZHOU HONG KONG MACAU

1939 1940 1941 1942 1943 1944 1945 1946 1947 1948 1949 1950 1951 1952 1953 1954 1955 1956 1957 1958 1959 1960 1961 1962 1963
1992 1993 1994 1995 1996 1997 1998 1999 2000 2001 2002 2003 2004 2005 2006 2007 2008 2009 2010 2011 2012 2013 2014 2020

with high density and pedestrian-friendly mixed-use spaces. The Guangzhou project tackled the challenges of design thinking and development strategies that deal with an accelerating rate of large-scale urbanization and suburbanization—two phenomena occurring simultaneously in China as the consequences of urban sprawl and economic growth. Both projects expose urgent contemporary issues related to the convergence of knowledge on physical urban design, the construction of architectural form, the formulation of planning policy, and operational real estate strategies.

The Boston site is occupied by a monolithic seven-story parking deck of 459,000 square feet, with an enclosed ground floor for retail. It is sandwiched between the Rose Kennedy Greenway and Boston Harbor, and surrounded by a mix of complexes built in the late 1960s and early 1970s; these include the New England Aquarium and two waterfront residential towers designed by I. M. Pei. The surroundings reminded us of the historical context of an era that sought to hide a formerly industrial waterfront from the sight of pedestrians. In dramatic contrast to this stark 1960s modernism is the mile-and-a-half-long, 15-acre linear public park of the Rose Kennedy Greenway, the result of the "Big Dig." When one of the largest and most technologically challenging infrastructure projects in the history of the United States achieved the removal of the elevated highway and redirected traffic into a tunnel system below the city, a new park was built on the reclaimed ground plane to link the city with its waterfront. The garage and its site were acquired in 2007 for $153 million, and they earn an annual net profit of $8.5 million for the developer.

The Guangzhou project, with an area of 21.48 hectares, is an urban redevelopment on a much larger scale; it is located on the banks of Haizhu Lake, along the north–south axis of the city's new central business district. The site is currently occupied by a network of small-scale, village-sponsored enterprises and service providers, with dilapidated houses and workshops lining two heavily polluted public streets. The course brief calls for the transformation of this inhospitable village into a livable urban district that can embrace the economic vitality of small-scale local businesses and provide a better livable environment for residents.

To offer a thoughtful design and development proposal, the students' explorations were not confined to the boundaries of the two sites. The horizontal and vertical dissection of the urban, historical, and economic contexts of the two cities increases both strategic possibilities and creative aspirations. Experiential and data-driven research each plays a critical role in helping students better understand the macro scale of the city's growth. For example, the illustrations included on page 11 and pages 19–21 are based on data collection and quantitative investigation of historical demographic density over time for Boston and the projected urban demographic aggregation for all districts of Guangzhou and its nearby regions. Page 19 represents the exploration of the gradual physical transformation of Guangzhou in relation to its geographic characteristics and shifting planning structure over the past two centuries. These three sets of diagrams together highlight the process of urban formation driven by multiple forces and indicate possible formal futures for the cities.

Guangzhou and Boston have long histories of shaping their respective cultures and built environments—Guangzhou over a span of 3,000 years, and Boston over 300. The two paintings on page 17 are persuasive in presenting their similar topography. The painting of Guangzhou dates back to 1800 and presents hills and oceans as natural features surrounding a densely built environment, dotted with Western-style buildings in the forefront and a pagoda in the background. The painting of Boston from 1732 depicts the hills looming in the background and the long docks extended into the sea, and churches with steeples visible throughout the city. These telling visual materials help us critically examine unique aspects of the formal origins of the two cities. Among the oldest cities in their respective areas, Boston and Guangzhou are currently grappling with different contemporary urban issues and creating innovative solutions.

Global Leadership in Real Estate and Design aims to generate new ideas and insightful strategies to help these cities envision their futures through thoughtful and interdisciplinary interpretation of specific sites: How to address the relationship between land and water? How to highlight the history and physicality of the sites? How to interpret dominant and long-standing typologies of the built forms, both old and new? And how to seize opportunities within urban transformation and growth and shape the built environment through a convergence of real estate and design? In so doing, the course hopes to identify the potential for redefining the parameters of each discipline, and thus strengthening their relations.

Leadership in Design

A. Eugene Kohn

Global Leadership in Real Estate and Design is unique in that it combines real estate development and architecture within a four-credit course at the Harvard GSD. I had the pleasure to teach alongside Bing Wang, who is key to the success of this course, for the second year in a row. Our course this semester was divided between two site-specific projects, each with a team made up of at least three members, including a real estate/business major and an architect (or planner or landscape architect)—not unlike the real-world relationships between an architect and a developer client.

In architectural design courses, students' work is typically judged by a jury on the merit of their creative design work. While this is certainly a vital element of architectural education, such reviews may not consider that in actual practice, a design is also shaped by external factors that are beyond a designer's aesthetic, the program, and the site. These additional factors include client goals for the project, the budget, and desired financial returns. Our Global Leadership course provides a basis for exposing students to the way they might actually practice as architects and real estate professionals.

The course included two projects of very different scales and contexts—one located in Boston and the other in Guangzhou, China—and the students visited the site to which they had been assigned. The program of the Boston project features a mix of uses, including retail, office, residential, hotel, and parking, on a 1.3-acre site. This site, referred to as Harbor Garage, is in a prominent location along the Greenway, well related to Long Wharf pier and adjacent to the Harbor Towers and the historically significant Custom House Tower. The project, consisting of approximately 1.2 million square feet of development with parking below, would replace a seven-story, 459,000-square-foot parking garage. The current garage produces a sizeable return of $9 million a year, which could discourage the owner from taking on the risk to develop any new building on the site.

While the Downtown Boston Waterfront project was located on a small site surrounded by historic buildings, the Haizhu Lake Ecological Village project is a 53-acre, mixed-use development including a wide variety of components. These components are primarily housing, from low-rise, single-family to multi-family, along with retail, hotel, and cultural facilities, and integrated transportation. The density and the ground-plane profile of this project prompted an enormous variety in the resulting schemes.

From my perspective, a major goal of the course was to teach students that good planning and design create value. I believe that there are three types of value in any project. Most obvious is value in a financial sense—value to the client or developer in creating a return on their investment that will continue to grow with time. A broader and more significant value is value to the users—in making a healthier, more enjoyable, and productive working environment for an office project, or a residential environment where people will have a better quality of life. The third value is one that extends beyond users to include value for a city—the quality and impact of a building and the external spaces created that affects those who

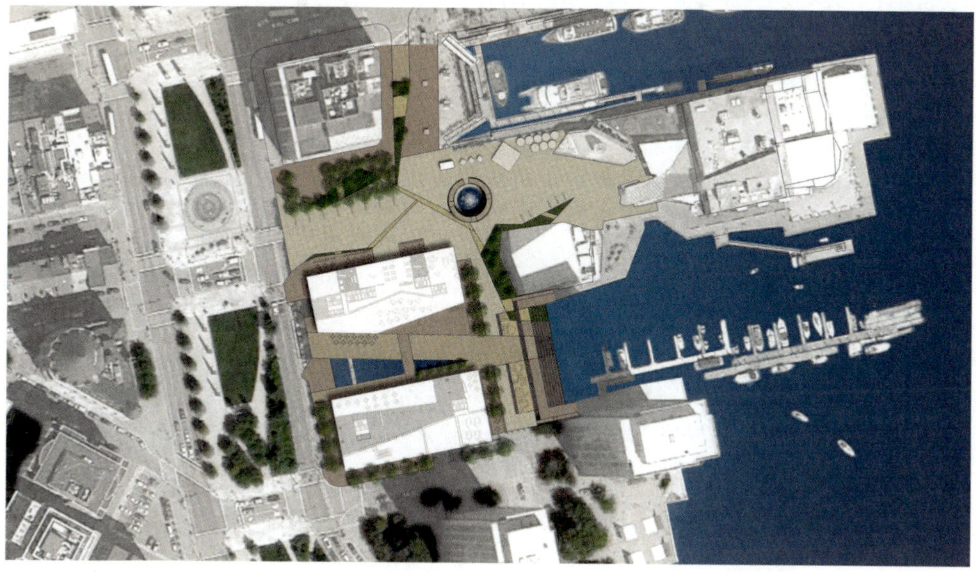

may not live or work in the development, but who experience it from the exterior, including its impact on the street and the sense of place it creates.

The architect's role is to create value in all of these senses: through the development of the programmatic solution, or function, and through quality of design, massing, and appearance. In this sense, these different definitions of value exist in a co-dependent relationship. For the most part, a building will outlive those who design and develop it, and can impact a city for many years. It is important that those responsible for the development, as much as architects, recognize this fact. Development and investment is not only about rate of return or amount of return, but about the value one creates for the city—for the people of the city. A thoughtfully designed building will attract tenants and garner higher rents, and can continue to do so for years.

My hope is that when our students enter the architecture and real estate professions, they will take what they learned in this particular course and apply it to their work, so they too can contribute to our cities and our built environment. A developer with great vision and creativity can lead a city's growth in the right direction by what he or she proposes and develops, and the architect can lead us as a result of the creativity and quality of what he or she designs. They together represent the global leaders in real estate and design. Such contributions set the standards for future development and growth, and the ideas spread to become global.

I attribute the success of this course to our students and Professor Bing Wang, who is the true leader of the course, as well as to our distinguished jurors ranging from architects to real estate developers to a famous architectural critic, both at mid-term and the finals, who applied their knowledge and experience to our students' work. Finally, it is our students who provided their creative solutions to these projects to be critiqued and judged, and for us all to learn from.

Building massing optimization and an open plaza are utilized as design strategies to connect the Rose Fitzgerald Kennedy Greenway and the Boston Waterfront in the Pivot proposal by Fabiana Alvear and Kyle Trulen.

Design Formulates the Next Wave in the Real Estate Industry

Sven Andersen and Thomas Schneider

Unlike most other sciences, the study of real estate at the graduate school level is still in the embryonic stage. Historically, graduate level coursework in real estate was a small subdivision of business programs or of architecture and urban planning schools. Whereas business school programs emphasize the financial and investment processes involved in real estate, MBA students typically lack adequate understanding of comprehensive real estate principles linked to other fields, such as design, construction, and soft factors that arise within the built environment. On the other hand, real estate courses at design and urban planning schools are often confronted with the opposite teaching challenge, and do not sufficiently cover the economics of real estate transactions.

Over the past several decades, the real estate industry has evolved into a discipline of great complexity with an increasingly institutional ownership structure. This increased complexity and internationalization of the industry has created a demand for practitioners with knowledge of real estate which extends beyond that of the traditional MBA generalist. This has led to the creation of new, one to two year graduate level real estate programs, which began with the founding of the NYU Real Estate Institute in 1967 (now known as the NYU Schack Institute of Real Estate) and shortly thereafter, MIT's Center for Real Estate (1983). In the following years, professional graduate programs or concentrations focused solely on real estate were established by Harvard University (1983), Columbia University (1985), the University of Southern California (1986), Johns Hopkins University (1989), and Cornell University (1996). These programs or concentrations emphasized a broader and evenly balanced education in real estate that recognized the complicated interrelationships between business, design, construction, and the built environment.

Unfortunately, the initial focus on holistic real estate education shifted during the last real estate boom, just before the housing bubble burst. The problem started with the concept of securitization applied to commercial real estate. This paved the way for potential misuse with far-reaching consequences for the industry. It created a marketplace for massive amounts of capital, desperate to be placed in this new growing field, which inevitably led to over lending. The financial sector's attempt to integrate real estate into their normal commodity trading business model compounded the problem due to the reliance on derivatives, and led to the eventual (and unfortunate) loss of any connection between the real asset and the security. The securitization boom had a marked influence on real estate programs, which were forced to incorporate these new products and topics into their curricula in order to maintain relevance and to meet the job requirements of the growing financial real estate industry. In addition, the tremendous success enjoyed by this new sector rendered the impression that highly attractive investment returns could be generated solely through creative financial structuring. Comprehensive knowledge of real estate itself and an understanding of significant external factors suddenly appeared obsolete to most real estate professionals in the finance sector.

The bursting of the housing bubble and the ensuing financial crisis acutely revealed that the financial industry had underestimated two main fundamental differences between real estate and traditional commodities such as oil, gold, or corn. The first and probably the more significant difference between real estate and other commodities is that real estate (land) is the only commodity that cannot be moved. This immobility of land places an inherent value on the location itself, while other commodities have limited locational values that are only determined by the cost of moving them to a favorable market. Unlike other movable commodities, land cannot be transferred from areas of surplus to compensate for areas where a shortage exists, which may affect both short-term and long-term investments.

The second difference between real estate and commodities that can be successfully traded is that commodities are not differentiated by producer. A barrel of oil is basically the same product, regardless of the producer. Compare this with real estate, where not only its quality and characteristics vary depending on the producer (or, in this case, the developer), but also its current and future value, depending on its locations and efficiencies of its management. In many regards, each building is even different from the one next door.

Together, these two factors reveal the real underlying problem of treating real estate like a commodity—each building is unique. It is important to clearly distinguish between real estate assets as unique, location-specific, hard assets with highly individual characteristics, and traditional securities or commodities. These two differences demonstrate the difficulty of standardizing and framing real estate so it fits into the financial service industry's commodities business concept.

The abovementioned complexities and unique characteristics of real estate should discourage the application of a simplified approach to real estate education and instead point to the adoption of a more holistic analysis of finance and investments so as to avoid market failures and inefficiencies. Graduate-level real estate education, be it academic programs or concentrations, that emphasize the built environment are even more important today, as we are living in a time in which rapid technological innovation is challenging and changing many of our long-established concepts. This evolution within real estate has occurred many times before.

One early example that clearly demonstrates the impact of innovation on real estate was the opening of the first Underground station in London in 1863. The Underground was built with the purpose of reducing traffic congestion in the city, but it additionally impacted typical commuting habits. The majority of people no longer needed to live within walking distance of their jobs, which had a knock-on effect on the requirements and concepts of the built environment of that time.

Today's innovations will likely have a similarly significant impact on the requirements of real estate in coming years. Technological advancement has already impacted the retail landscape by decreasing the number of stores and changing their formats. The same holds true for the office market, where mobile technologies have influenced how companies plan for and occupy office space to accommodate new ways of working.

These changes present both risks and opportunities. Real estate professionals that are able to understand and properly respond to these new trends will be able to generate superior alpha returns and outperform their competitors.

A holistic educational approach with emphasis on design appears to be the best practice under the current market conditions. This will not only enable future real estate practitioners to understand and correctly evaluate the impact of various innovations on their product, but will also encourage them to shape or redesign properties in the best possible way to fit today's consumer demands. Overall, the complexities of real estate presented here illustrate the necessity of embracing multiple influencing factors in order to properly assess how to deal with the challenges of today and those of the future. For these reasons, we believe that returning to a more holistic real estate education with an emphasis on design and the built environment will provide real estate practitioners with the best tools to tackle challenges and create opportunities, and will bring positive long-term effects on the real estate industry over the coming decade.

Place and Profit: Assessing the Plans of Global Leadership in Real Estate and Design

Blair Kamin

A skyscraper "must be every inch a proud and soaring thing."
—Louis Sullivan

A skyscraper is "a machine that makes the land pay."
—Cass Gilbert

The conflicting declarations of these two great architects encapsulate the tensions that ripple through the Harvard Graduate School of Design course led by Professors Bing Wang and Eugene Kohn. Global Leadership in Real Estate and Design provides a significant alternative to conventional design studios, which are based on the notion that architecture school is a time to experiment, unrestricted by the confining pressures of real estate development and land-use economics. While there is much to recommend this approach, Professors Wang and Kohn bid students to simultaneously take into account both the investors' desire to achieve profitable returns and peoples' aspirations to live, work and play in settings attuned to their climates, customs and culture. With real estate capital coursing around the world as never before, this brief has never been more relevant. It requires a more complex form of creativity than a typical design studio, one that seeks to resolve the conflicting mandates of form and finance, place and profit. The best student work for this class, prepared for sites in Boston and the large southern Chinese city of Guangzhou, meets the demands of this difficult brief.

The two sites are a study in contrasts, not only due to the difference between the widely varying, four-season climate of New England and the subtropical monsoon climate of southern China. The Boston parcel is a 1.3-acre Downtown plot occupied by a profitable, 1,000-space parking garage which blights the city's historic waterfront as well as the adjacent Rose Fitzgerald Kennedy Greenway. The Guangzhou property, an outlying 21.48-hectare parcel along a lake, sits a few kilometers south of the city's new business district. The district, known as the Pearl River New Town, is packed with skyscrapers by famous architects yet it is devoid of vital urbanism. At the same time, certain characteristics link the Boston and Guangzhou sites: both occupy potentially lucrative waterfronts, which, to varying degrees, reflect the transformation of such properties from industrial-era eyesores to showcases of post-industrial recreation and culture. Both sites also have been targeted by business and political leaders for new uses and transformative physical change. Indeed, the Boston site's contested character reveals another way in which Global Leadership in Real Estate and Design departs from conventional teaching models.

Just weeks before the students were to present their final plans, the city's new mayor, Martin J. Walsh, dismissed the aversion of his long-serving predecessor, Thomas Menino, to the presence of tall buildings along the Rose Fitzgerald Kennedy Greenway. The new mayor's attitude—"How tall can you go?"—provoked predictable controversy in a tradition-bound city

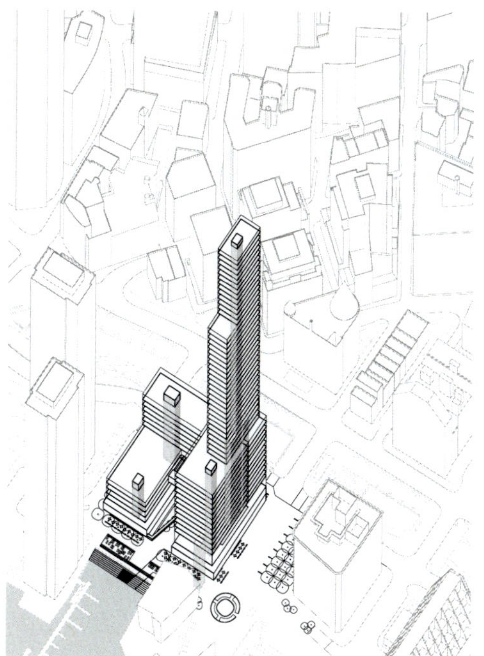

whose residents, it is said, have made a blood sport out of hunting down and killing bold architectural plans. When Kohn's firm, New York–based Kohn Pedersen Fox Associates, released renderings of its two-towered plan for the site in July 2014, residents of a neighboring high-rise complex termed it "historically and contemporaneously inappropriate in scale, height, and density for a location adjacent to two Boston treasures, the Rose Kennedy Greenway and the Harbor." This criticism added a layer of political tension to the form-versus-finance conundrum their students already faced. With a highly politicized public review process a given, key questions arose: What would the designs give to the city? What would they take? The project, it became clear, had to deliver more than an iconic architectural statement. It had to upgrade the public realm, offering a trade-off: more density and height in return for better public space. Adding to the exercise's real-world character, the project's developer, Donald Chiofaro, sat on the final jury.

After initial struggles, the Boston students broadened their vision beyond real estate pro formas to sophisticated urban design, with the team of Alessandro Boccacci, Dylan Lazovik, and Ying Zhang achieving the most dramatic shift. Their mid-term plan, which called for a single massive hotel and condominium tower, showed little awareness of Boston's rich tradition of fine-grained architecture and place-making urbanism. Their final design retained the original economic program, but creatively reordered it in the form of two mirror-glass towers joined by occupied, bridge-like floors that formed a monumental gateway to the waterfront. The parking garage, sensibly, had been pushed underground. To be sure, this scheme was an unpersuasive architectural hybrid—a modernist abstraction of the John Hancock Tower married to the tradition-inspired postmodernism of Rowes Wharf. But the students had honed in on several attributes of Boston-specific urbanism: thin skyscraper massing that related well to the nearby Custom House Tower, an entrance to the Waterfront that would be animated by public art and stores, and lot-line architecture that framed the surrounding public spaces.

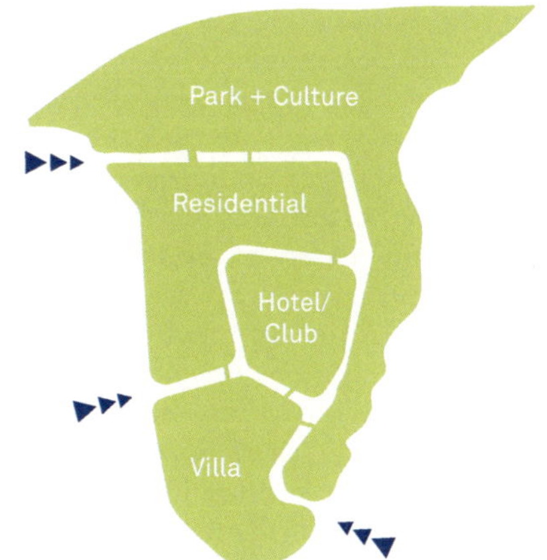

Even better was the plan by Fabiana Alvear and Kyle Trulen, which called for a mix of offices, condominiums, shops and a hotel. The students' careful study of Boston architectural precedents, their lucid examination of skyline massing, and such politically savvy moves as a shadow study lent their plan an aura of elegance, even of inevitability. Two towers, the taller one an attractive thin slab, would be split by a public space leading from the Greenway to a tiered waterfront plaza. The proposed passageway would incorporate such enlivening details as glass ceiling-panels that would tantalizingly reflect the waters of the harbor. They even elevated that most utilitarian of building

Left: Two towers, the taller an attractive thin slab, would be split by a public space leading from the Greenway to a tiered waterfront plaza, as depicted in the axonometric drawing by Fabiana Alvear and Kyle Trulen for the Pivot proposal.

Right: Art River proposal actively engages the water as an urban Rightdesign element to construct programmed islands and distinct neighborhoods. Art River diagram by Luis Gil, Christine Min, and Han Wang.

types—the underground parking-garage—to something with a measure of aesthetic stature. One end of their garage contains a column of water that would shoot past the cylindrical ramps leading visitors to the surface. Such people-friendly landscape architecture, combined with the students' place-sensitive urbanism and elegant tower silhouettes, make this scheme a model of creative commercial design.

Similar challenges confronted the Guangzhou teams, though their task was considerably more difficult. The Boston teams, after all, were only a few subway stops from their site, a proximity that allowed the students to deepen their knowledge through repeat visits. Their Guangzhou counterparts, in contrast, had just a few days to take in their site in the Haizhu Lake District and were therefore vulnerable to the blind spots that inevitably result when architects and urban planners are "parachuted in." During mid-term reviews, most of the designs fell prey to this trap, with one exception: a plan by the team of Luis Gil, Christine Min, and Han Wang. Their proposal brought water from the perimeter of the site to its center, inserting a series of canals that split the prosaic parcel into uniquely shaped islands linked by bridges. An expensive idea? Undoubtedly. But waterfront property always sells for a premium, which gave the plan strong aesthetic and financial appeal. Though not without faults, like a planned circular hotel that strove to be a civic icon but looked imposingly isolated, this scheme effectively escaped the trap of "parachuted in" placelessness.

Its insights were developed in impressive ways by the final plan of another team—Patrick Boateng, Matt Ciccotti, and Brian Vargo. They suggested slicing 13 canals, inspired by those in the ancient Chinese city of Suzhou, through the lower two-thirds of the parcel. They thereby ensured that every residential unit would border on water. Instead of generic open space, they offered a rich diversity of green spaces, from active athletic areas to serene botanical gardens to intimate tea gardens. Rather than quoting from the past, the design was inspired by it. Like the praiseworthy Boston projects, the design exemplified the virtues of "critical regionalism," at once respecting the character of its site and bringing something new to it. As summarized by the image of a canal boat gliding past planked walkways, lush foliage, and contemporary homes whose overhangs would provide shelter from the sun, the outcome revealed a persuasive integration of the public and the private realms, form and finance, the aspirational architecture of Louis Sullivan and the hard-edged pragmatism of Cass Gilbert.

This is the lasting lesson of the Global Leadership in Real Estate and Design course: it is possible, though certainly not easy, to resolve the conflicting demands of the drive for profit and the ethical imperative to create a spirit-lifting sense of place.

The Haizhu Gardens proposal by Patrick Boateng, Matthew Ciccotti, and Brian Vargo embodies virtues of Critical Regionalism in the master plan and architectural design strategies.

Project I

Mediating Between Static and Fluid Urban Systems

Guangzhou, China

Thoughts and Reflections: Developing Leadership in Real Estate and Design

Brian Vargo, MDes REBE

What is leadership? Real estate development involves innumerable factors—technical, cultural, political, and more. How do we lead competing interests in the same direction?

This course began with that simple question, posed to 30 of us in our first meeting. Representing a wide variety of nationalities, professional skill sets, and academic focuses, we proposed vastly different definitions with surprisingly little overlap. Eventually our discussion gravitated toward some common themes, ranging from a mastery of communication and mindfulness of a team's dynamics to exceptional talent and commitment to innovation.

From the beginning of the course, our task was to escape a simple methodological practice of real estate development and to consider how this open question could influence our academic trajectory. Dividing the class roughly in half, the course focused on two projects within entirely different contexts, and almost incomparable in scale and context. The juxtaposition of the two underscores the importance of fostering an approach to real estate development rather than seeking a simple solution to two design problems. The course is neither a design studio nor a real estate class; it requires a knowledge of both design and financial practices, but also an investigative process that reaches beyond those seemingly parallel worlds. Our task was to develop an approach to real estate development on a global scale with a critical perspective.

This groundwork formed the basis of our development process. Our group of three focused on the 52-acre plot adjacent to Haizhu Lake in Guangzhou, China. The first challenge lay in grasping the scale and the context. Our initial impressions of the physical site were limited; there was only so much we could learn from grainy Google Earth images.

Our conceptualization of a master plan began long before a particular design ideology emerged. A master plan on this scale requires a thorough understanding of its context—political, cultural, and financial. While we were limited to a single site visit halfway through the project's development, research from afar could fill gaps in our understanding. For the first few weeks, we studied the problem in layers, uncovering greater levels of detail concerning adjacent land uses, transit systems, and development precedents. We scoured all available resources, wandering in scale from the history of city planning in Guangzhou District to the specific cultural identity of Haizhu Lake. Perhaps our most pressing concern, an apparently simple one, was to determine the scale of building that would be appropriate for the site. Our design sketches juggled floor-area ratios that ranged from 0.25 to 4.0, as if they were interchangeable. A realistic approximation of the scale and the building typologies that would constitute the master plan seemed elusive.

Our analysis of the local property market and investment conditions proved to be the most insightful tool in addressing those persistent questions. While Guangzhou continues to grow at a breakneck speed and on a magnificent scale, the overarching market trends point in a few clear directions. The market for office space, for example, is saturated with recently completed unabsorbed floor area. Retail and hospitality developments offer some potential, although there are caveats in their successful implementation. The market for residential real estate is a clear front-runner. Whether traditionally owned apartments or service apartments oriented towards short-term or long-term rentals, China's macroeconomic trends drive a seemingly unfettered demand. An analysis of market precedents also revealed the scale at which we could operate. Given this development context, it could be plausible to add 100,000 square meters (a million square feet) in a single phase of construction. While this is nearly unprecedented in contemporary developments elsewhere, we projected that the local market could absorb around a thousand units of dense housing on our site within a year.

These development metrics may seem banal, but they informed a vocabulary to articulate the master plan that was otherwise unfamiliar, and a strategic overview that preceded the bulk of our design process. Outlined in broad strokes by our research, a vision of a mixed-use residential district and a thematic anchor emerged in collective discussions. Without having visited the site, we felt increasingly cognizant of its contextual opportunities, physical and otherwise.

Nevertheless, place-making requires a narrative of physical spaces beyond the level of research. What urban concept would engender not just a series of buildings but a comprehensive development strategy that gives substance to these otherwise abstract conditions? How can the global application of real estate development be understood at the human level?

The site visit, which had been planned to take place halfway through the course, provided the means to inspire that overarching narrative. We were already armed with a thorough knowledge of the context and this enabled us to be strategic in our investigation of the site. Our questions were pointed and precisely targeted. What were the opinions of the local planning authority's initiatives? What sort of functions would be expected to take place in the public spaces? Given local variables, were the assumptions we used to underwrite our financial modeling realistic?

Collecting detailed information on Haizhu Lake was just as important as our experiences in other parts of Guangzhou. While international market reports were useful in some respects, a ten-minute conversation with local experts revolutionized our understanding of the site and its context. In Guangzhou we met with a series of local developers working at various scales in the city and elsewhere in China. We toured other recent development projects that offered precedents for our site, but also meandered through older parts of the city to get a sense of its cultural lineage. We noted local tactics in designing for south China's climate as well as the constituents of the residents' daily lives. This engendered a sense of place and an understanding of the people that a project of this scale touches.

On returning from this site visit our team felt inspired. As we discussed the problems and opportunities we had encountered, a development narrative emerged that seemed natural and strategic on both the urban design and financial levels.

Implementing that narrative proved to be a difficult task. As with every group in the course, we were from completely different backgrounds: I had trained as an architect and the other two members came from real estate appraisal and public policy. Carrying our collective vision forward would require balancing our talents, but we had no common professional perspective or medium for communication.

It is essential to find that medium where ideas can evolve collectively. A successful development project at this scale cannot simply assemble a set of components. It needs to evolve in iterative cycles that incorporate a wide array of perspectives and information in pursuit of a common strategy. While we could discuss the same project and its solution in principle, it would require a carefully orchestrated process for the details to fall into place and to deliver a meaningful proposal.

To achieve this we used two media that marched hand-in-hand: a master plan and a pro forma. They were codependent, and the interchange of numbers between the two was essential to understanding the physical and financial dimensions alike. While this approach was at first cumbersome, we found that we could understand more easily the impact of design decisions on the financial model, and vice versa, by plugging in the numbers and viewing the two simultaneously. At some point, the two components started to inspire one other. For example, the need for product differentiation in the project's real estate strategy resonated with the desire to draw variety in the design of various housing options. The master plan's fundamental structure divided buildings by ownership structure, making the project attractive to international investors. Thematic landscape elements of our project diminished buildable floor area, but higher sale prices clearly justified their design by creating a net benefit.

A wide variety of productive decisions emerged from this dialogue, although it was sometimes evident that a design decision could not be justified in financial terms. Likewise, the financial perspective sometimes determined aspects of the urban design in ways that were clearly not ideal. While both perspectives enriched the development process tremendously, they have fundamentally different metrics. Our focus was not simply on optimizing each decision, but rather on remaining faithful to the larger vision. At the end of the day, a development project must function as a single, cohesive strategy that embraces several tactics. If some decisions could lend value to that narrative in spite of being suboptimal individually, they were still best from a strategic perspective when considering that comprehensive vision.

As the course approached its final weeks, the various projects coalesced into remarkably different identities. While all the teams in the class started with approximately the same conditions, a variety of strategies emerged, each with its own merit. This was particularly interesting when considering the Boston and Guangzhou projects together. We did not discuss design or financing decisions idiosyncratically, but rather the application of various comprehensive development strategies.

Perhaps the context of global real estate development and the inherent difficulties of approaching a problem that lies outside a known context makes one more acutely aware of each step—or potential misstep. The 15 weeks that we spent developing our projects felt uncertain. In hindsight, the nature of that investigative process was essential in forming enduring principles of any project across boundaries.

A project of this scale requires a careful balance between team members, outside influences, and internal ambitions. It requires the understanding of an undefined problem through two different lenses—real estate and design—and finding a solution that reconciles the two within a defined set of parameters. In reference to the course's opening discussion, leadership in real estate design and development is the maintenance of this balance. It is a commitment that lends meaning to a comprehensive vision and requires persistent navigation through a labyrinthine process. Leadership in real estate development does not reside in any single approach, but rather in the cultivation of this collective process.

Multidisciplinary team members of Global Leadership in Real Estate and Design course perform site investigation and due diligence research in Guangzhou, China.

Articulating the Programmed Ecosystem: The Haizhu Gardens

Patrick Boateng II, MUP / MPP
Matthew Ciccotti, MDes REBE
Brian Vargo, MDes REBE

04 Situated along the Pearl River Delta about 75 miles northwest of Hong Kong, Guangzhou is the third largest city in China. After emerging in the 1970s as a major manufacturing center, the city has more recently refocused its development efforts on turning itself into an international metropolis and financial center.

We started by approaching the site as a wetland environment and searching for an understanding of how urban development can take place within such a context. The Chinese city of Suzhou is a particularly fitting precedent, given the environmental and cultural terrain the Haizhu Lake development will inhabit. Suzhou developed from a wetland ecology by building an extensive system of canals and is now known as the "Venice of China." The city's waterways create a rich urban fabric in which the qualities of the natural environment and the built environment are integral. After studying the technical aspects of the Suzhou canals, we proposed the creation of 13 canals on the Haizhu site, ranging in size and character, that would provide view-corridors into the land mass. This will result in an urban fabric in which every building is bordered by water, and where the canals can contribute to the local water management system. Just as the wetlands have shaped the physical environment of Haizhu Lake, so too will they shape its architecture.

The system of canals divide the site into a rich variety of neighborhoods, and their programming and design is therefore

“The opportunity to design a major urban development in Guangzhou should take on a critical perspective of this legacy.”

of utmost importance. Haizhu Lake is essentially a large, unprogrammed public park. We proposed to breathe life into the site with the Haizhu Gardens, an imaginative series of 55 gardens tailored to the public vision for the district. While each will be unique in design, together they will constitute a series of episodic experiences to give the site a unified identity.

Our overall development strategy consisted in developing the site with a 65 percent loan-to-cost construction loan, which would be paid off with condominium sales in years four and five. At the same time, once the income-producing portion of the site is stabilized (in year five), we would take out a permanent loan (75 percent loan-to-value), the proceeds of which could be used to pursue other projects and pay off investors. We would hold the income-producing portion for three to five years to demonstrate strong performance, and sell that portion to institutional investors in year ten. With this structure, the before-tax internal rate of return (IRR) with the project-level leverage is 26 percent, which we feel would be sufficient to attract a significant amount of interest from domestic and international investors.

SOURCES & USES: PROJECT COST AND CAPITAL ALLOCATION

USES	CNY (¥)	PSQM (GROSS)	USD ($)	PSF (GROSS)	%
Land Acquisition	1,086,750,000	8,513	175,000,000	127	34%
Hard Costs	1,445,278,069	11,321	232,733,989	169	45%
Soft Costs	271,055,614	2,123	43,648,247	32	8%
Contingency	160,133,368	1,254	25,786,372	19	5%
Leasing	124,762,097	977	20,090,515	15	4%
Financing	139,493,650	1,093	22,462,746	16	4%
Total Development	3,227,472,798	25,281	519,721,869	378	100%

¥ 1 CNY = $ 0.16 USD (May, 2014)

CAPITAL USE

CAPITAL STACK

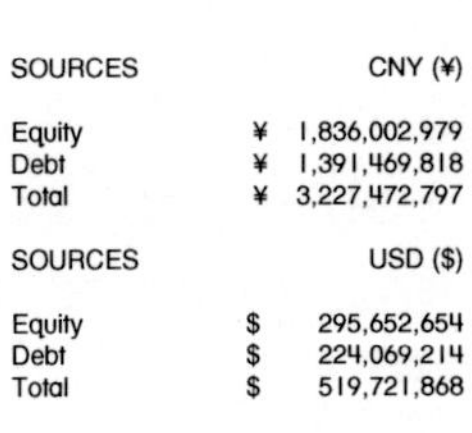

SOURCES		CNY (¥)
Equity	¥	1,836,002,979
Debt	¥	1,391,469,818
Total	¥	3,227,472,797

SOURCES		USD ($)
Equity	$	295,652,654
Debt	$	224,069,214
Total	$	519,721,868

¥ 1 CNY = $ 0.16 USD (May, 2014)

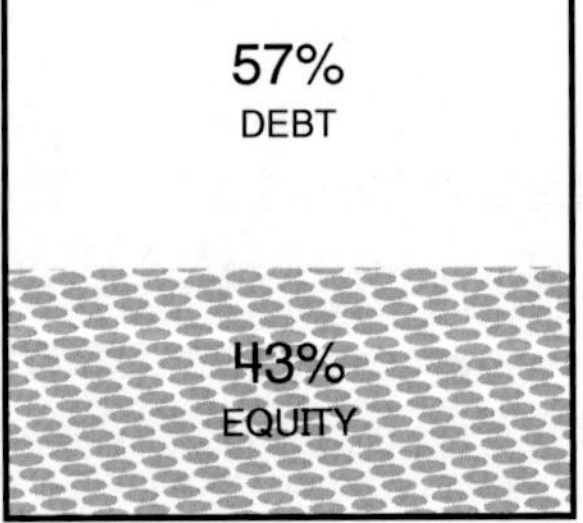

Above: The projected development costs and capital allocations funded by a balanced combination of debt and equity.

Following page: The Haizhu Gardens master plan is designed as a network of episodic experiences that range in activity level and programs to create a vibrant waterfront urban ecosystem.

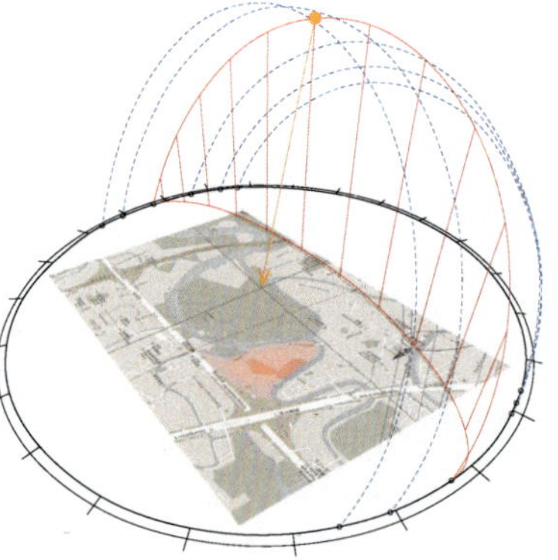

Solar Analysis

Solar Altitude

66.6° March 21 at Noon

89.8° June 21 at Noon

43.4° December 21 at Noon

Annual Gross Horizontal Irradiance

1255 kWh/sqm

Top: To create a richly textured environment, the open space system resonates on a variety of levels and configurations responding to the local climate, including the urban scale, the public and private landscapes, and the pedestrian experiences.

Following page: The central feature of the proposal's open-space network is a large outdoor amphitheater ringed by public functions that anchors the development to the adjacent metro stop.

HARD COSTS SUMMARY

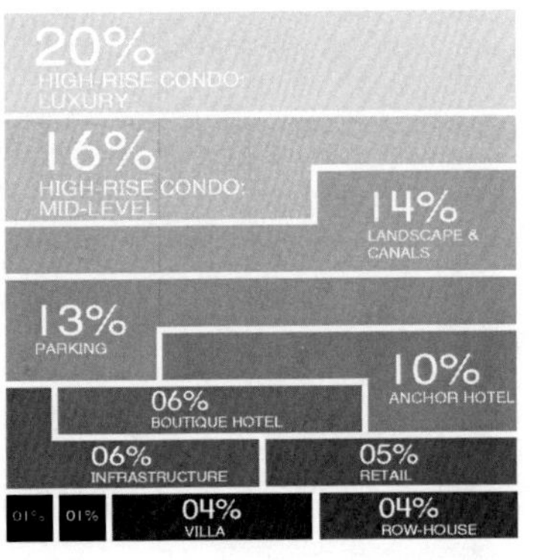

CONSTRUCTION COSTS

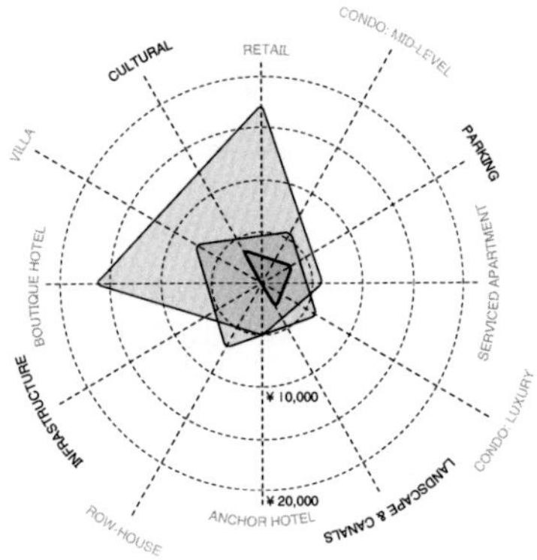

HARD COSTS BREAKDOWN (CNY + SQM)

Use	Gross Area SQM	Hard Costs CNY ¥ / SQM	Hard Costs CNY ¥	% of Total
Retail	11,561	6,000	69,366,000	5%
Serviced Apartment	4,200	5,000	21,000,000	1%
High-rise Condo (Mid-level)	42,900	5,500	235,950,000	16%
High-rise Condo (Luxury)	49,260	6,000	295,560,000	20%
Rowhouse	9,431	6,500	61,301,500	4%
Villa	6,826	7,500	51,195,000	4%
Anchor Hotel	8,885	16,000	142,160,000	10%
Boutique Hotel	5,360	17,000	91,120,000	6%
Cultural	800	4,000	3,200,000	0%
Parking	55,550	3,500	194,425,569	13%
Infrastructure	n/a	n/a	80,000,000	6%
Landscape & Canals	100,000	2,000	200,000,000	14%
TOTAL*	127,662	11,321	1,445,278,069	100%

*Gross Area does not include open space, below-grade retail and parking.

¥ 1 CNY = $ 0.16 USD (May, 2014)

Above: The boutique and anchor hotel programs are projected to have the highest construction cost per square meter.

Following page: Canal system divides the site into distinct neighborhoods with specific programs, creating both view corridors and a common amenity that drives value at multiple scales.

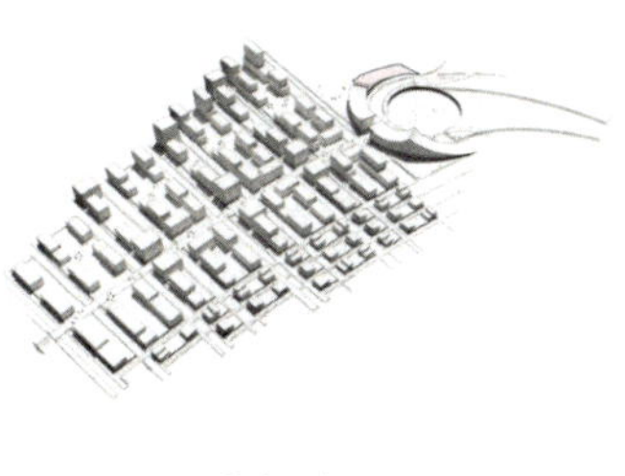

Cultural

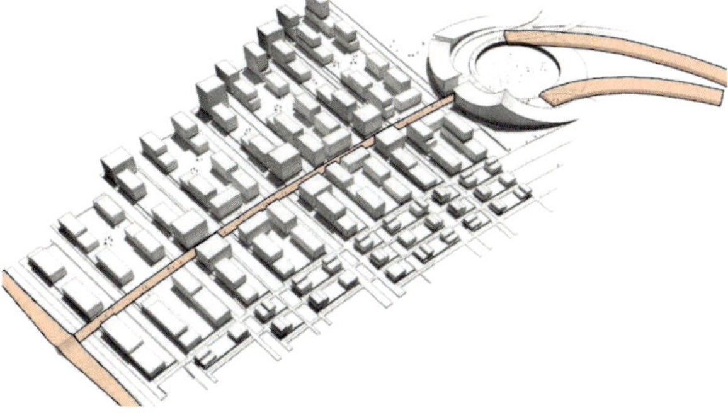

Retail

CHARACTERISTICS		COSTS		RETURN PARAMETERS	
Gross Area (SQM)*	11,561	Hard Cost (¥ / SQM)	6,000	Rent (¥ / M / Day)***	21.37
Efficiency Factor	95%	Soft Cost (% of Hard)	20%	Rent Growth Factor	3%
Net Area (SQM)	10,983	Contingency (% of Hard)	10%	Vacancy Factor	15%
Average Unit Size (SQM)	500	Total Cost (¥ / SQM)	8,580	OpEx Ratio	15%
Number of Units	21	% of Unleveraged TDC	3%	Terminal Cap Rate	7%

*8,561 SQM Gross is below-grade

***Blended overall market rent

Hotel: Boutique

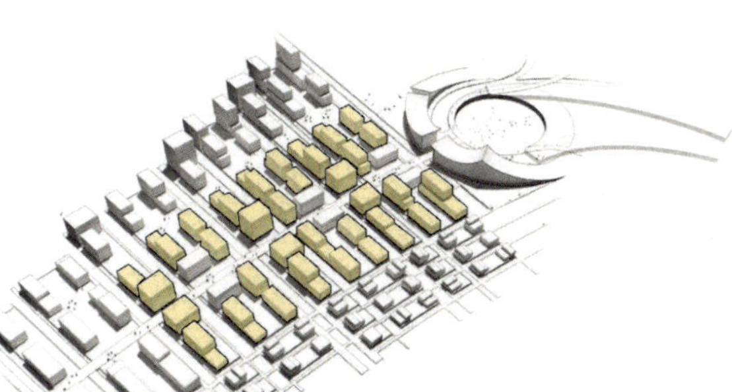

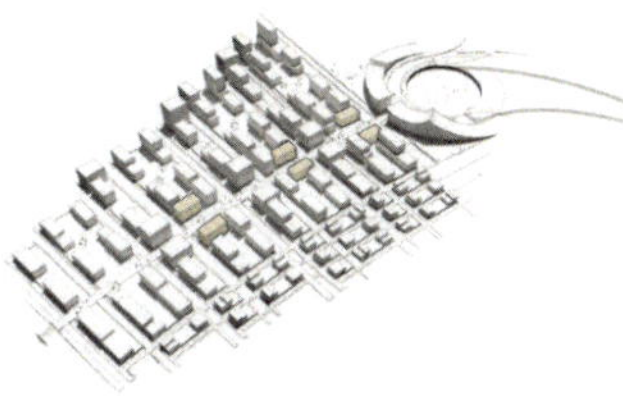

Residential: Serviced Apartments

Residential: Luxury Condo

CHARACTERISTICS		COSTS		RETURN PARAMETERS	
Gross Area (SQM)	49,260	Hard Cost (¥ / SQM)	6,000	Price (¥ / SQM)	42,500
Efficiency Factor	85%	Soft Cost (% of Hard)	20%	Rent Growth Factor	3%
Net Area (SQM)	41,871	Contingency (% of Hard)	10%	Sellout Period (Years)	2
Average Unit Size (SQM)	125	Total Cost (¥ / SQM)	9,075	OpEx Ratio	n/a
Number of Units	334	% of Unleveraged TDC	13%	Profit Margin	79%

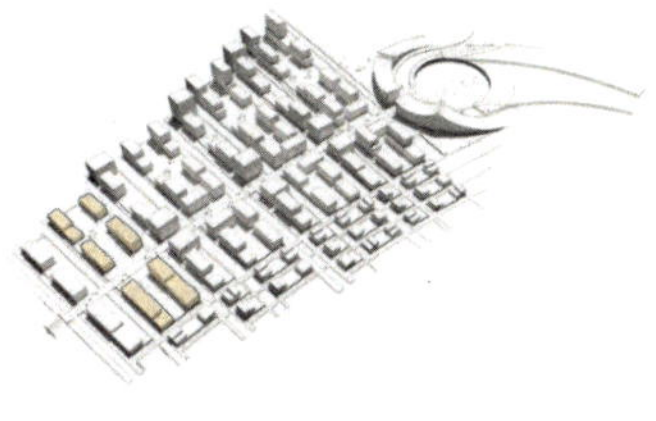

Residential: Rowhouse

Urban Stratification: Augmented Eminence

Stefan Di Leo, MAUD
Aaron Locke, MDes REBE
Terry Lu, MDes REBE

Haizhu Lake is a wetland lake within the larger Wanmu National Wetland Park, which occupies more than 71,700 hectares at the center of Haizhu District. The site challenges planners, developers, architects, and landscape architects with complex existing conditions and issues that demand a solution addressing the environment, form, ecology, finance, and culture, as well as community development. A particular challenge, proposed by the local planning authority, is to revitalize, celebrate, and embrace the vernacular Lingnan landscape and agriculture, with the intention of making the site a key cultural destination for the district and the city.

Our project is a mixed-use development on a 22-hectare site, implementing a design strategy to maximize both the open space and the allowable FAR (floor-area ratio) while providing a unique walking, shopping, and living experience through the superimposition of spatial and programmatic land forms, buildings and massing-heights. Conventional building layouts proved ineffectual in providing optimal views and privacy for the residential units and also resulted in a dull pedestrian experience. The advantages of the terraced volume are twofold: to establish a distinctive and varied walking experience with constant changes in building heights and the direction of view sheds, and to free up as much surface as possible for open green space by condensing the building volumes.

"Design strategy is to maximize both the park space and the allocated FAR while providing a unique walking, shopping, and living experience."

By agglomerating uses on the eastern part of the site, incorporating big-box retail, and placing villas and the clubhouse on the terraced roof of the structure, a higher FAR was achieved without sacrificing quality. As proposals for this site have a history of opposition from regulatory authorities, special attention was paid to the wishes of the municipality. The scheme extends Haizhu Park beyond its current boundaries, providing an additional 18 hectares of open space, and maintains the required 200-meter setback to the north. Terracing the building to the east mitigated concerns about the view from the park, which is screened from the full expanse of the development.

The project itself would be a SPV (special purpose vehicle) for purposes of liquidity, with an initial equity investment of CN¥ 1.1 billion and a 70 percent LTV (loan-to-value ratio) at 6.5 percent for five years. Condominiums, serviced apartments, and villas would be sold during a two-year period, while the hotel and retail would be sold separately, en bloc, in 2020 with a combined capitalized value of CN¥ 5.8 billion. The entire project, from investment to exit, would be completed in seven years, and would yield an unlevered and levered return of 33 percent and 47 percent, respectively.

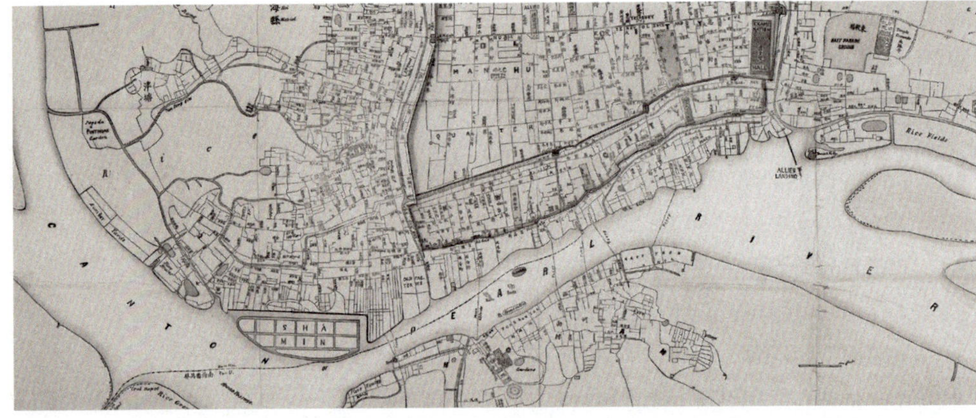

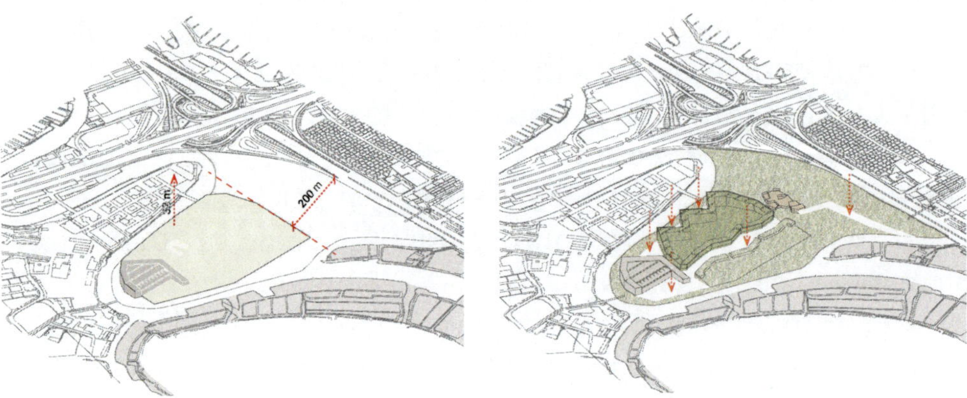

Top: An 1860 map of Canton (Guangzhou) showing the integration of the city structure with the tributaries of the Pearl River.

Above, left: The project's urban massing strategy based on the 200m setback and existing hydrology. Right: Articulated programmatic volumes are generated based on operations of "carving" to create opportunities to inject water as an integral feature of the site.

Following page: The development scheme engages the landscape elements as strategies to organize the master plan.

PROGRAM COMPOSITION

CONSTRUCTION COSTS (¥/SQM)

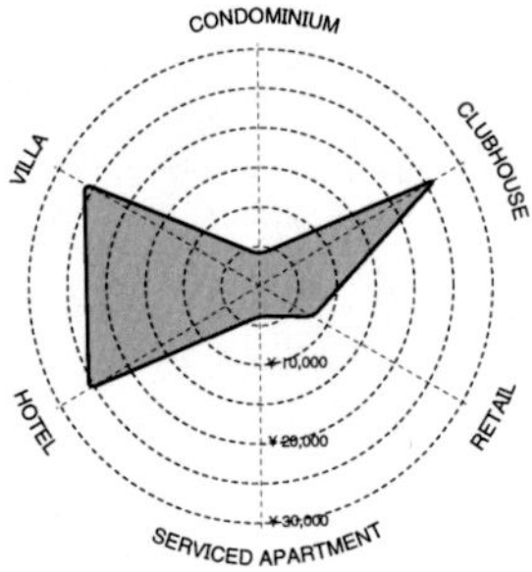

CAPITAL STACK

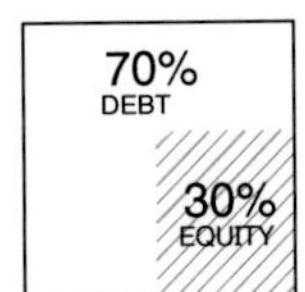

Total Development Cost	¥3,715,783,639
Loan to Value Ratio (LTV)	70%
Loan Amount	¥2,601,048,548
Interest Rate	6.5%
Loan Term	5 Years
Interest Only	
Monthly Payment	¥ 14,089,013
Annual Payment	¥ 169,068,156

¥ 1 CNY = $ 0.16 USD (May, 2014)

PROGRAM SUMMARY

Program	Gross SM	Efficiency	Net SM	FAR	Units	%	Parking Spaces
Condominium	46,290	85%	39,347	0.21	393	18%	79
Serviced Apartment	47,759	85%	40,595	0.21	406	18%	81
Retail	108,119	95%	102,713	0.48	-	42%	1,081
Villa	15,600	100%	15,600	0.07	14	6%	20
Clubhouse	2,800	100%	2,800	0.01	-	1%	14
Hotel	32,621	65%	21,204	0.14	300	13%	163
Cultural Center	5,000	100%	5,000	0.02	-	2%	50
Total Building	258,189		227,258	1.15		100%	1,489
Less Under Ground	(13,012)						
Total Development	245,177		258,766	1.09			

PROJECT DEVELOPMENT SCHEDULE

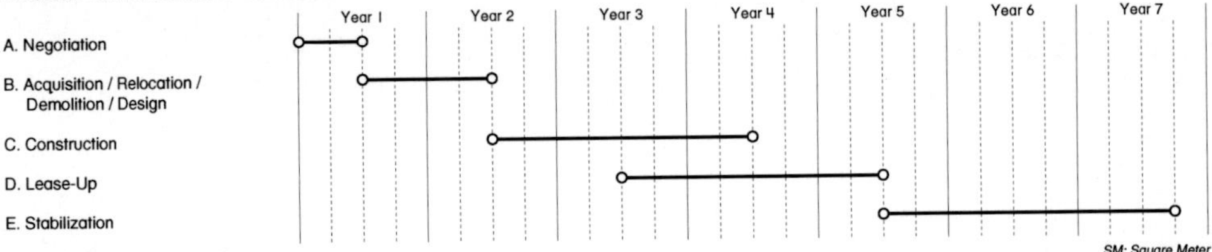

SM: Square Meter
FAR: Floor Area Ratio

Above: The financial strategy is proposed to reach stabilization by year five and to exit the project by year seven.

Following page: Comparison of a typical and Tiantang Ding development scheme comparison illustrates the potential for optimization of the project through integrated design.

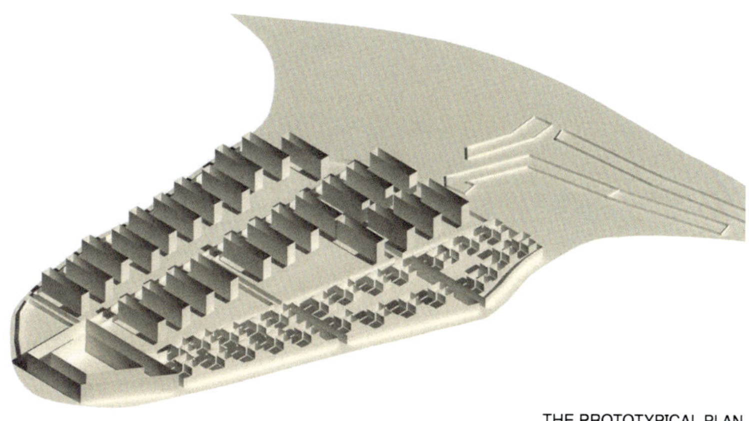

THE PROTOTYPICAL PLAN

Total Cost:	¥ 3,577,700,000
Gross SM:	297,600
% of Open Space:	51%
Unleveraged IRR:	27%

¥ 1 CNY = $ 0.16 USD (May, 2014)
SM : Square Meter
IRR : Internal Rate of Return

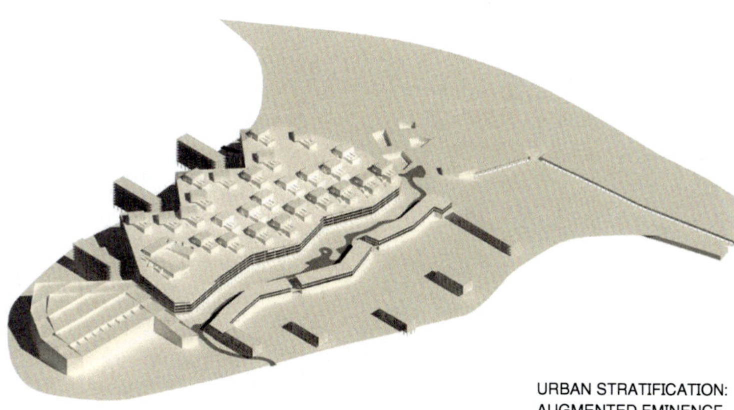

URBAN STRATIFICATION:
AUGMENTED EMINENCE

Total Cost:	¥ 4,525,550,000
Gross SM:	297,600
% of Open Space:	80%
Unleveraged IRR:	33%

¥ 1 CNY = $ 0.16 USD (May, 2014)
SM : Square Meter
IRR : Internal Rate of Return

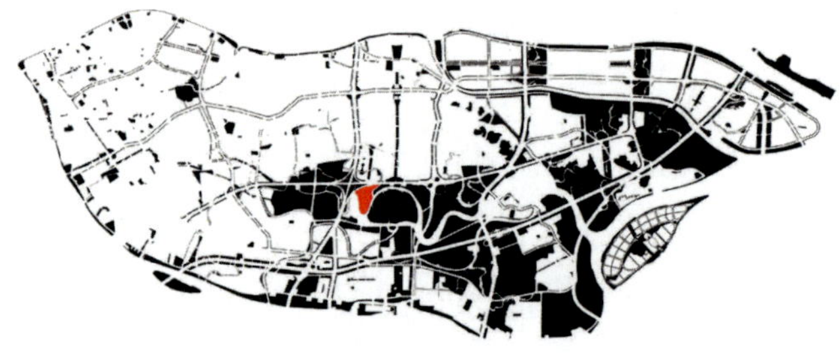

Top: Haizhu Lake and its open space are connected by a north–south axis to the center of Southern Guangzhou.

Bottom: Pastoral open space typology celebrates the synthesis of modern and historical qualities.

Following page: The stacking of programs toward the southern tip of the site enables greater density of uses to maximize allowable FAR and area for open space.

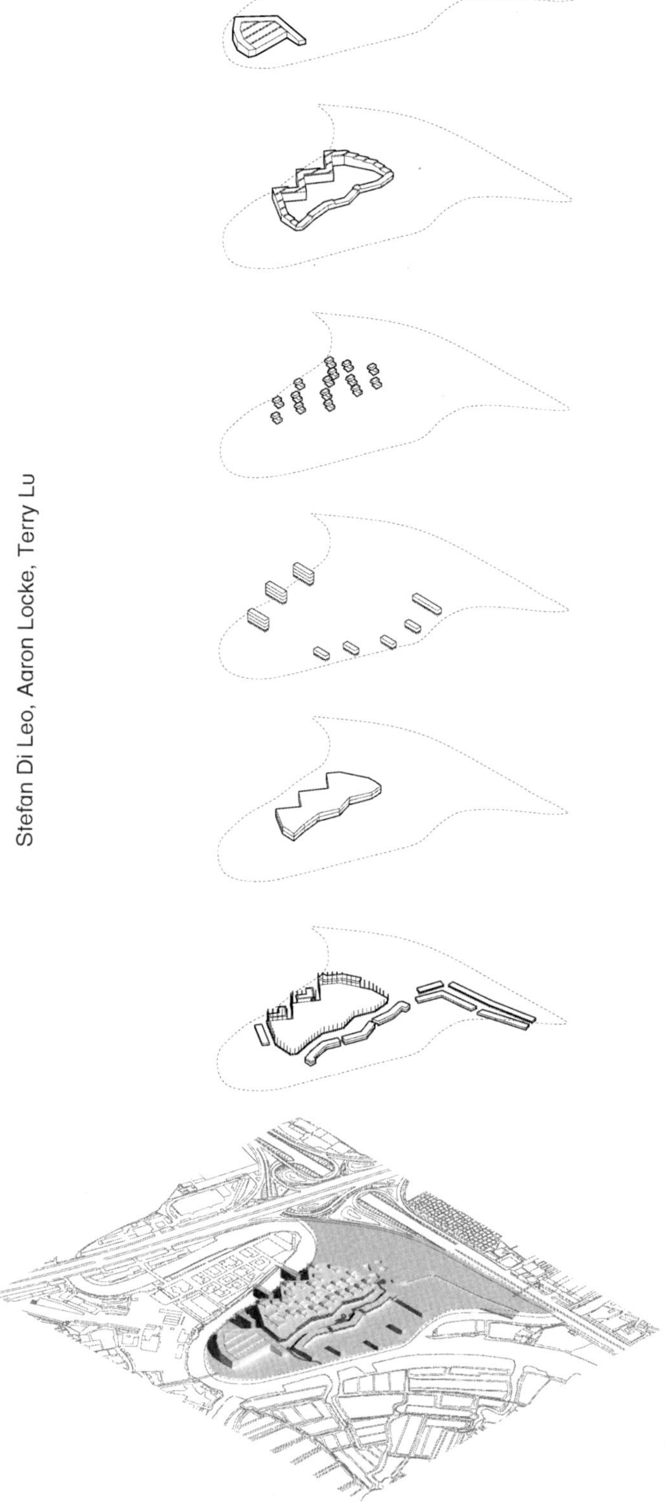

HOTEL	
Gross Square Meter	32,621
Floor Area Ratio (FAR)	0.14
Units	394
Construction ¥ / Square Meter	¥ 20,053
Gross Construction Cost ¥	¥ 654,159,743
Average Daily Rate	450
Occupancy	70%
Annual Gross Revenues ¥	¥ 396,733,000

SERVICED APARTMENT	
Gross Square Meter	47,759
Floor Area Ratio (FAR)	0.21
Units	478
Construction ¥ / Square Meter	¥ 3,676
Gross Construction Cost ¥	¥ 175,583,299
Price ¥ / Square Meter	¥ 3,676
Average ¥ / Unit	¥ 5,013,333
Gross Revenues ¥	¥ 2,191,137,348

VILLA	
Gross Square Meter	15,600
Floor Area Ratio (FAR)	0.07
Units	52
Construction ¥ / Square Meter	¥ 20,053
Gross Construction Cost ¥	¥ 312,831,979
Price ¥ / Square Meter	¥ 90,240
Average ¥ / Unit	¥ 103,775,993
Gross Revenues ¥	¥ 1,485,951,901

CONDOMINIUMS	
Gross Square Meter	46,290
Floor Area Ratio (FAR)	0.21
Units	463
Construction ¥ / Square Meter	¥ 3,342
Gross Construction Cost ¥	¥ 154,711,456
Price ¥ / Square Meter	¥ 46,791
Average ¥ / Unit	¥ 4,679,111
Gross Revenues ¥	¥ 2,463,050,503

BIG BOX RETAIL	
Gross Square Meter	41,000
Floor Area Ratio (FAR)	0.21
Construction ¥ / Square Meter	¥ 6,684
Gross Construction Cost ¥	¥ 274,044,000
Rent ¥ / Square Meter	¥ 2,350
Annual Gross Revenues ¥	¥ 72,349,200

RETAIL	
Gross Square Meter	108,119
Floor Area Ratio (FAR)	0.48
Units	Varies
Construction ¥ / Square Meter	¥ 6,684
Gross Construction Cost ¥	¥ 722,715,401
Rent ¥ / Square Meter / Year	¥ 2,350
Occupancy	95%
Annual Gross Revenues ¥	¥ 66,634,250

¥ : Chinese Yuan / Renminbi
¥ 1 CNY = $ 0.16 USD (May, 2014)

Top: High-density urban superblock with bisecting thin slab towers and promenade.

Bottom: Elevation of garden housing typology at waterfront with terraced roof villas in background.

Above: Optimized densification strategy enables spatial, economic, and environmental synergies.

Following page, bottom: The design-integrated development strategy is projected to have a high internal rate of return for equity.

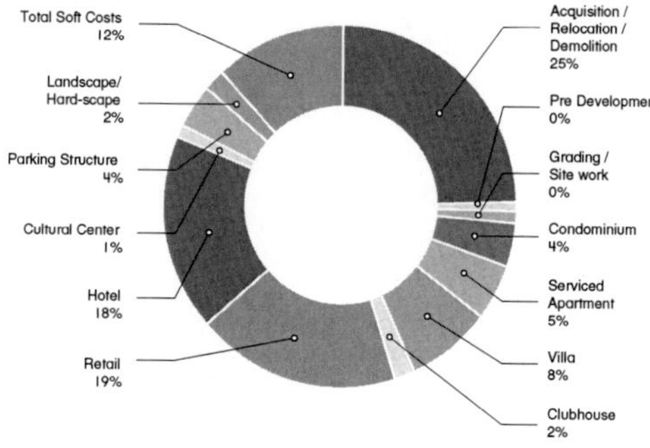

RETURN MEASURES

Total Project Cost	¥ 3,715,783,639	$ 598,354,853
Unleveraged IRR	33%	
Equity	¥ 1,114,735,092	$ 179,506,456
Leveraged IRR	47%	

EXIT CAP RATES

Hotel (2020)	7%
Retail (2020)	6%

¥ 1 CNY = $ 0.16 USD (May, 2014)
IRR: Internal Rate of Return

Burgeoning Iconic-ism in Vernacular Urban Conditions

Aaron Locke, MDes REBE

In a city over 4,000 years old, with a population of 14 million and an area of 2,870 square miles, the sheer scale of Guangzhou is iconic.[1] Beyond this are multiple facets and degrees of urbanization interwoven over generations, from the fishing village of the Spring and Autumn Period, through the period of the Lingnan culture, and expanded over the last millennium. Guangzhou has adapted to accommodate the rapid shift in socioeconomic conditions, requiring significant vernacular interventions. Recently, it has seen tremendous economic and population growth that has required an unprecedented sequence of developments, creating iconic urban conditions. The objective here is to explore a small fraction of these conditions from three outlooks: briefly from a historical perspective, retrospectively from a transitional and romanticized utilitarian standpoint, and critically with regard to recent urban interventions.

Traditional Architectures

The remnants of Cantonese design and tectonics from the Lingnan culture can still be seen in Guangzhou today. Narrow streets, high stone walls, pitched tile roofs, and intricate wooden details embody the essence of the style. More subtle but equally significant is the connection to water, as can be seen in the Lingnan Impression Garden, a full-scale replica of a town, located south of Guangzhou University Mega Center. Here, the connection is fabricated through a small stream that bisects the promenade and flows into the second of four small lakes. A more visible reminder of Guangzhou's past are the Qilou buildings found on commercial streets such as Shangxiajiu Lu and Zhongshan Lu, where long arcades directly adjacent to the street provide shelter from the unpredictable showers and sunlight for which Guangzhou is known.[2]

The "Village in the City"

Guangzhou has since sprawled to its fringes, filling the voids between factories with "villages in the city"—a dense urban fabric woven of concrete, erected vernacularly in response to an urgent demand for housing. These mounds of battered concrete lack proper plumbing, adequate circulation, and natural light. Often owned by landlords living off-site, these squalid buildings provide shelter for the city's less affluent population. However, the accelerating sweep of development has lately brought towering apartments to the edge of these "villages in the city."[3]

Just as Haussmann choreographed in Paris, and Moses in New York, Guangzhou is "cleansing" itself of this urban mix to make way for the repetitious, the infringing, and the grandiose. The city has abandoned its historic core and defined an idealized location for a new central business district, seemingly irrespective of the existing context. Eminent domain is used to aggregate large amounts of land for aggressive infrastructural and commercial development. Larger economic and political drivers help to spur this development, which is undeterred even by declining vacancy rates following an unprecedented delivery of office space. Concurrently, the ephemeral "village in the city," an iconic and arguably historical typology, is vanishing.

The New Guangzhou

Above the ruins of the "village in the city," a new icon emerges. Its gleaming neon lights illuminate the Pearl River. The towers and cultural centers of the new central business district bring a host of attributes that contribute easily to the iconic urban condition. Hierarchy is apparent in multiple facets throughout. A north–south axis is weighted at both ends, with the Guangzhou East Railway Station to the north and Canton Tower to the south. A large portion of the central axis is occupied by a public park, promenade, and underground shopping district. This amenity provides enormous value for the adjacent parcels, and institutes an additional hierarchy between the "park-front" towers and the neighboring structures beyond. Two of the most prominent office towers in the central business district, the IFC and, currently under construction, CTF towers, frame Canton Tower and act as a visual gateway. Cultural programs are given prized waterfront locations. The children's museum, opera house, library, and art museum form a cultural square at the water's edge, outplaced only by the Asian Games Venue on Haixinsha Island.[4]

Guangzhou's reliance on and connection to the Pearl River has given it prominence as a source not only of visual stimulation but of an experiential and emotive connection. The river's position as a gateway to Guangzhou accentuates the optical effects of light and water, and connects the city to the Pearl River Delta.

The more recent typology of the garden city has allowed the infiltration of public parks and open spaces, creating a more humane ratio between city and landscape while also allowing water to penetrate the urban fabric. The programmed open space is most notable along the new central axis and is slated to be extended south from Canton Tower, terminating at Haizhu Lake, known by locals as the "lungs" of the city. Little of the park is occupiable, as it is more a lake than a park. A sliver of land that circumvents the park's interior is sporadically covered in assorted vegetation and trinket shacks. Nevertheless, it is visited by a million visitors a month, the prime location and ease of accessibility by metro making it a more popular destination than the large expanse of preserved land to the east.

Anticipation of the traffic congestion that would result from the modernization of Guangzhou, coupled with a desire for natural light among the skyscrapers, has led to the creation of immensely wide boulevards. Although necessary, these new streets of the central business district may not be entirely friendly to pedestrians, who are often faced with long swathes of blank walls or sterile underpasses, as urban superblocks neglect streetscapes in favor of internal amenities. Crossing the city is hindered by an inconvenient public transport system and is typically easier by cab or motorbike.

Conclusion

Although economic conditions may be pointing toward more stable growth patterns in the near future, the level of aspirations for the redevelopment of Guangzhou shows no signs of abating. Through its own deep historical roots, intervention from abroad by means of trade, and current economic and social changes, Guangzhou has acquired both laudable and abhorrent urban contexts and conditions. These, regardless of how they are perceived, are reconciled by the waters that flow through city. Lucidly, the streams of the Lingnan promenade and the Canton Tower on the edge of the Pearl River deduce this pining connection. Less notable are the arcades of the Qilou buildings, erected out of the necessity to provide shelter from rain. Guangzhou's current campaign to eradicate the "village in the city" is in fact removing a typology that lacks even the most necessary of hydrodynamic infrastructure. As can be seen in what has come to fruition of late, Guangzhou is a city of transformation, but its waters remain in focus.

Notes

1. "Guangzhou Population Closes to 15 million," Guangzhou International, http://english.gz.gov.cn/publicfiles/business/htmlfiles/gzgoven/s4171/201105/809843.html.
2. "*Lingnan* Culture," Guangzhou International, http://www.gz.gov.cn/publicfiles/business/htmlfiles/gzgoven/s9133/201104/789737.html.
3. Yanliu Lin, Bruno de Meulder, and Shifu Wang, "Understanding the 'Village in the City' in Guangzhou: Economic Integration and Development Issues and Their Implications for the Urban Migrant," *Urban Studies 48* (2011).
4. Bing Wang, "Global Leadership in Real Estate and Design" (course description, Harvard University Graduate School of Design, Cambridge, MA, Spring Semester 2014).

Composing the Productive Eco-Lifestyle

Zhewen Dai, MLA I
Jason McAlees, MDes REBE
Frankie Refuerzo, MUP / MDes REBE

The city of Guangzhou is famous for its water, cuisine, flowers, and orchards. The site itself, next to a beautiful but generic park surrounding Haizhu Lake, had a potential to counterbalance the super urban development scale that is common throughout the city. We set out, to create a healthy place with multiple facets—environmental, physical, social, and financial.

The land-use plan separates the public uses of the site—a mixed-use retail and residential corridor, a botanical garden, and a hotel with its associated amenities—from the private residential area. Our plan for open space is organized along a large central spine connecting smaller neighborhood open spaces, in an effort to create a beautiful and healthy landscape and enhance the value of interior spaces that might otherwise be difficult to market.

We envision Haizhu Gardens as a counterbalance to the predominant development patterns in contemporary China—dense and hyper-urban. Our focus on creating a healthy place permeated every element of our site and our strategy, including the selection of uses, site programming, the provision of public amenities, and analysis of regulatory constraints.

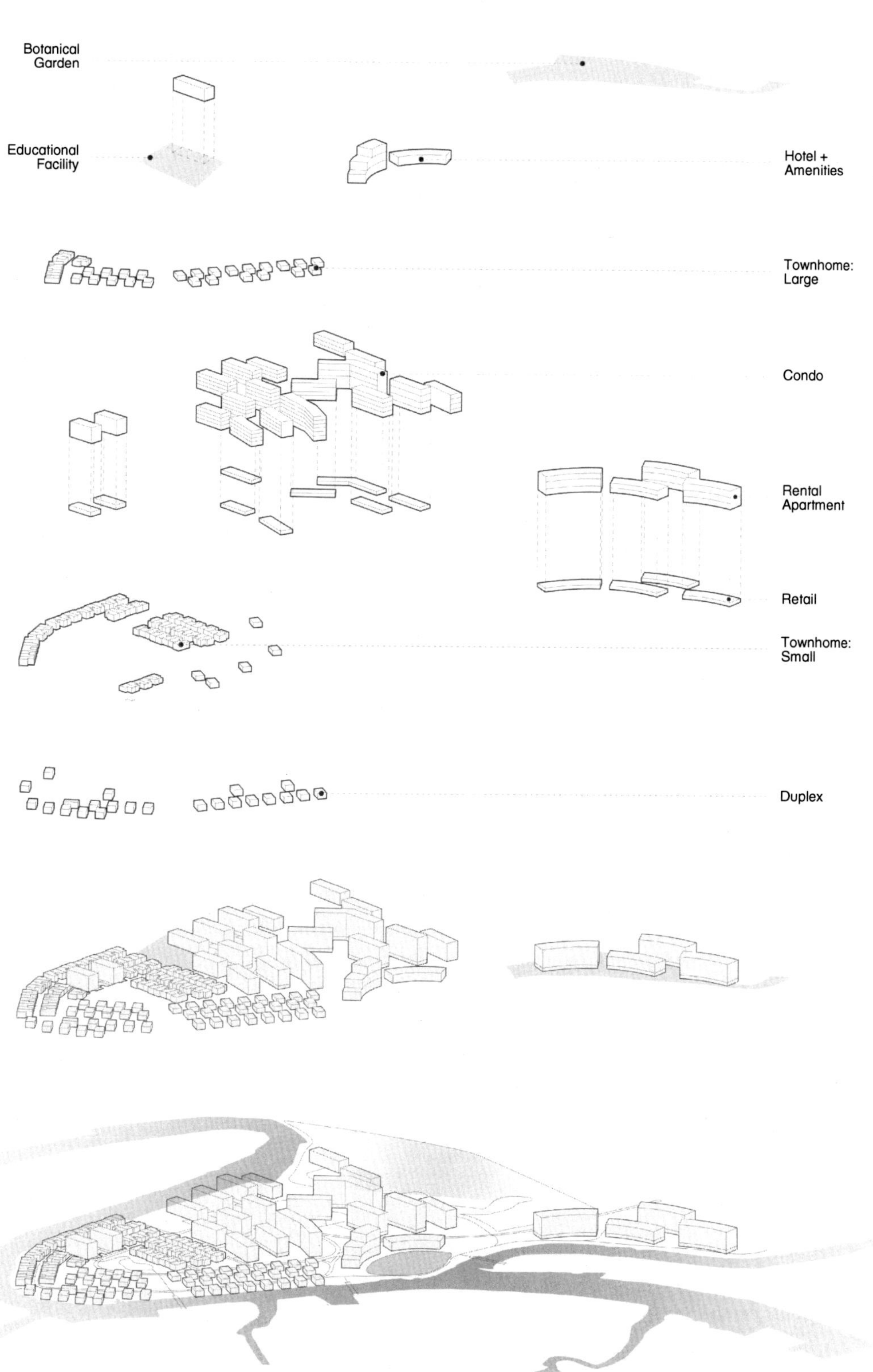
Botanical Garden
Educational Facility
Hotel + Amenities
Townhome: Large
Condo
Rental Apartment
Retail
Townhome: Small
Duplex

PROGRAM COMPOSITION

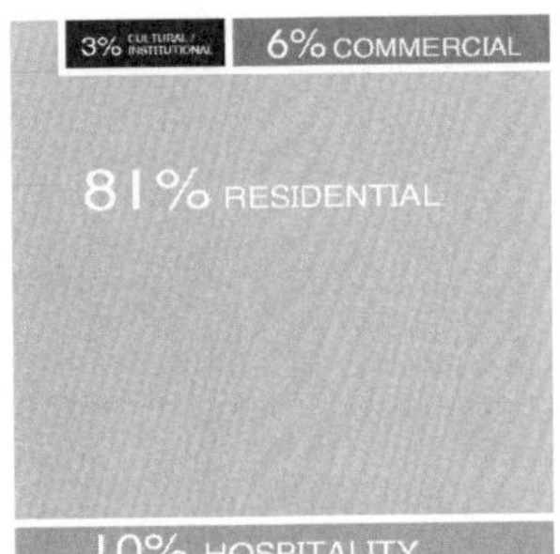

RESIDENTIAL HARD COSTS
(USD/SF)

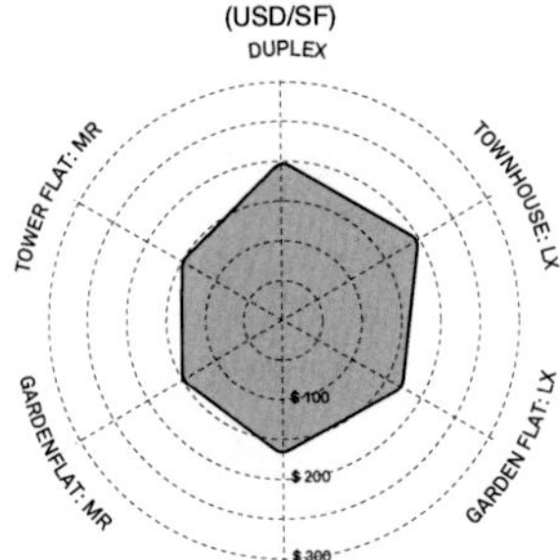

RESIDENTIAL PRICE PER SF
(USD/SF)

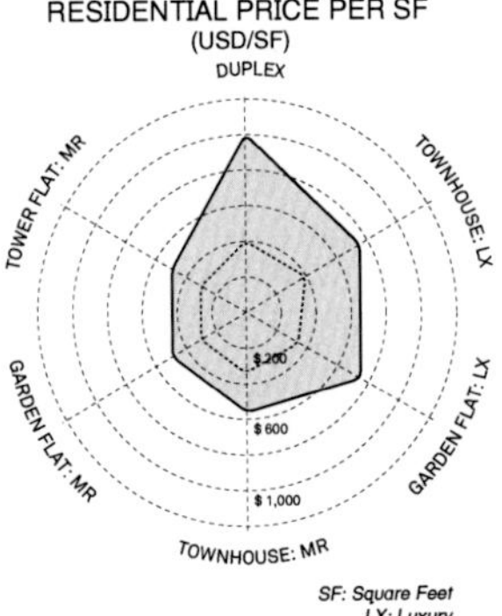

SF: Square Feet
LX: Luxury
MR: Mid-range

PROGRAM SUMMARY

Program	Gross SF	Average SF	Units	Hard Cost (USD/SF)	Price (USD/SF)
■ Cultural / Institution	50,000	-	-	-	-
■ Commercial / Retail	101,000	-	-	-	-
■ Hospitality	164,900	-	-	-	-
■ Residential	1,361,570	-	-	-	-
Duplex	66,500	3,500	19	200	1000
Townhouse: Luxury	73,000	1,932	87	150	753
Garden Flat: Luxury	148,000	1,247	6	125	750
Townhouse: Mid-range	168,070	1,987	36	125	547
Garden Flat: Mid-range	277,000	961	252	100	500
Tower Flat: Mid-range	455,000	732	552	100	500
Village Rental Apartment	174,000	-	533	100	-
Total Development	2,312,088		1,485		

SF: Square Feet
FAR: Floor Area Ratio

Previous page: Eight different residential typologies catering to diverse age and income demographics compose 80 percent of the development. The typologies vary in size, location, construction cost, materials, and price. The diversity generated through the typologies introduces a healthy diversity in ages and incomes.

Above: The program composition focuses on intermixing 8 distinct residential typologies and public programs to promote the dynamic juxtaposition of socially active, economically productive, and healthy lifestyles.

Following page, top: The separate circulation systems allow diversity of spatial experiences focused on a productive lifestyle with an emphasis on nature. Bottom: The waterfront is reserved for public open space that highlights Haizhu Lake's ecological beauty while offering respite from city life and subtropical heat. Open space network plan is rendered to depict watercolor effects.

Pedestrian Circulation Waterway Pattern Vehicular Circulation

Art River: Typological Archipelago

Luis Gil, MDes REBE
Christine Min, MArch II
Han Wang, MAUD

In a city with more than 8 million residents, Haizhu Lake offers respite from the dense development of Guangzhou. The expansive man-made lake, canals, and surrounding orchards are a popular amenity in the congested city, a moment of tranquility in an otherwise bustling urban center. The Art River development takes its cue from the contextual waterscape and is proposed as an interconnected archipelago.

Art River proposal's program composition consists of a residential, hotel, and retail development, as well as a cultural center and a sculpture park. These programmatic elements are conceived as interconnected islands organized by a canal system that is an extension of the existing waterways of Haizhu Lake. The canal system has a dual function: to provide physical separation of specific programs and to increase the length of the valued waterfront. Furthermore, the canals and the island communities are designed to embody and reflect specific architectural and natural contextual qualities.

A 117-key hotel complex anchors the center of development and functions as a core program and a logistical hub, providing service amenities for the surrounding development. To the south of the hotel complex are residential villas that are serviced by the hotel but are sold as individual residences. Taking their organization from the road grid of the historic Haizhu area of Guangzhou, the villas are arranged as series of perimeter block houses with

"Physical programmatic elements are conceived as interconnected islands organized by a canal system that is an extension of the existing waterways."

shared courtyards, a typology that was inspired by the traditional Chinese courtyard house.

This development proposal enhances the site's inherent potential by maximizing the value of the existing waterscape. The proposal's seamless integration with the existing built environment and creation of a distinctive development product recognize the importance of a tranquil quality of life that is provided by Art River.

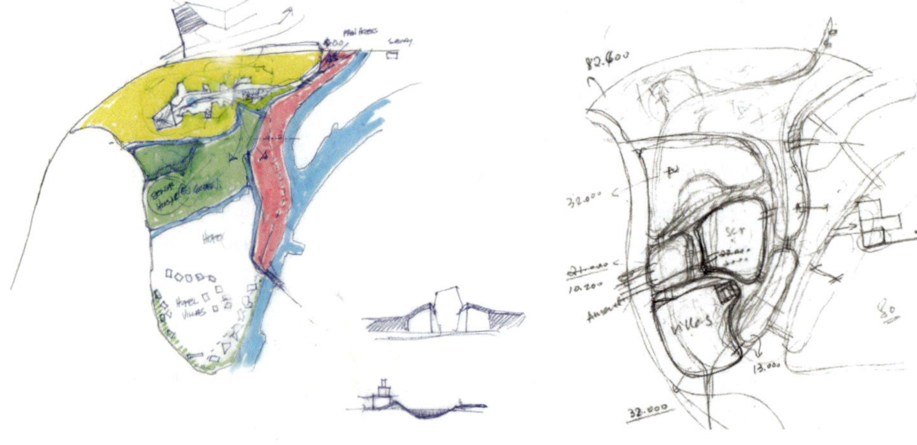

Above: The formation of a programmed archipelago derives not only from urban and natural contexts but also from its financial feasibility.

Following page: The distinct qualities of each programmed island are articulated through each island and canal's form, internal urban structure, and building typology.

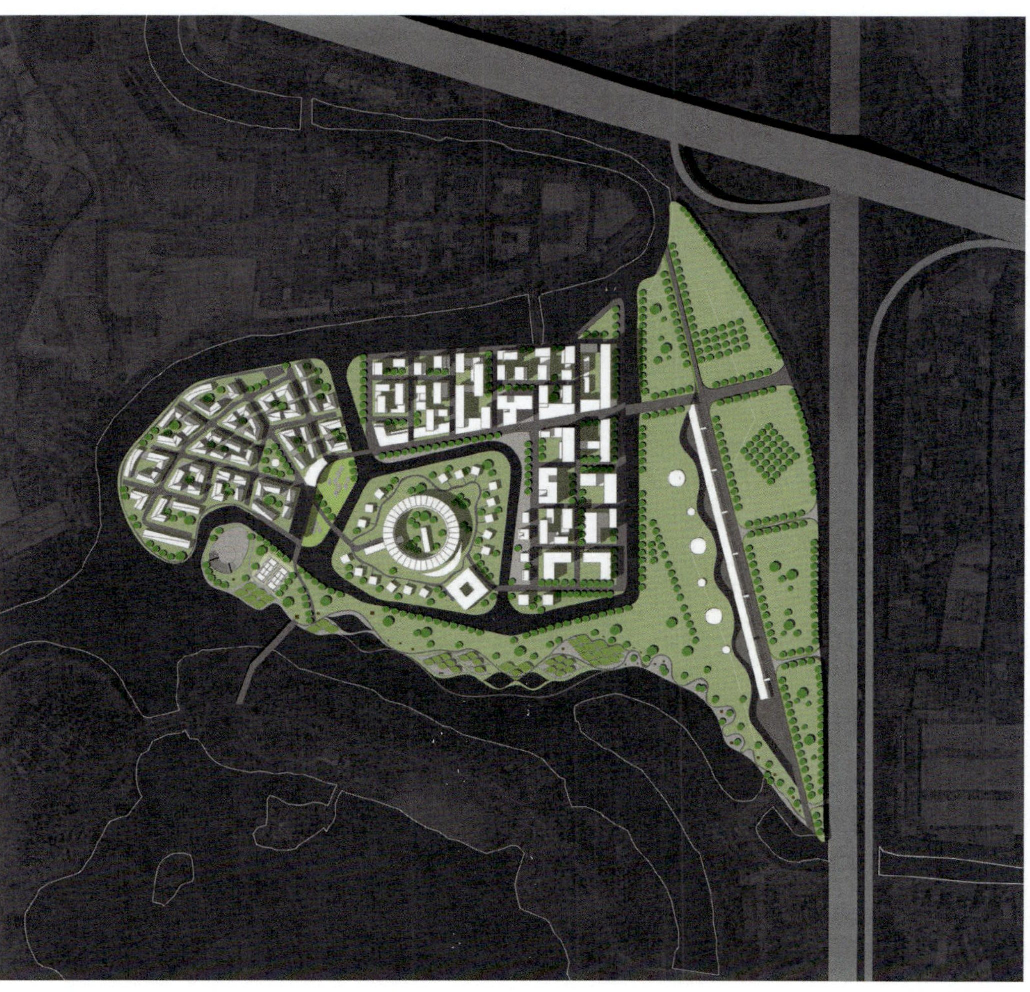

Art River: Typological Archipelago

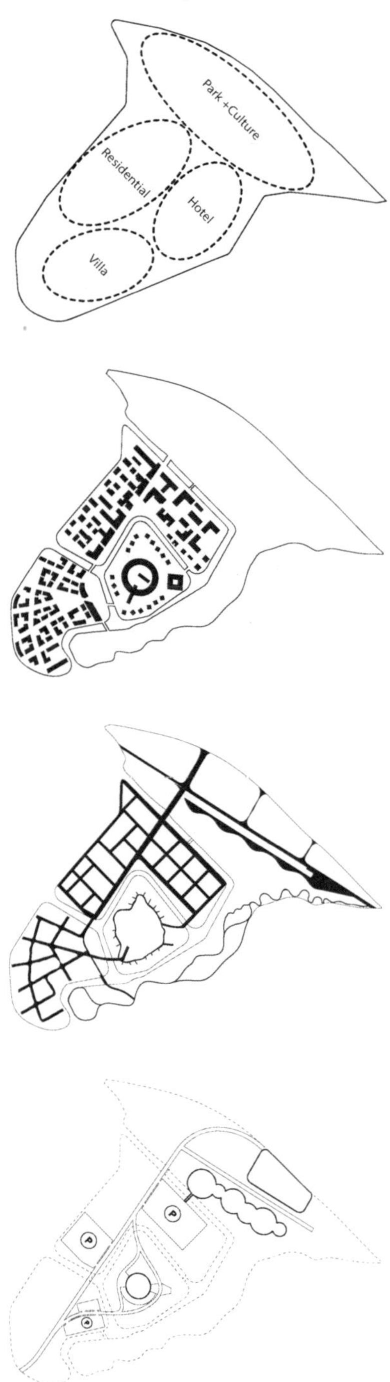

Previous page: Green spaces are a dominant component of Art River's quality of life.

Above: 1. Program distribution and allocation based on site attributes. 2. Figure-ground diagram of above-grade buildings on site. 3. Above-grade vehicular and pedestrian circulation diagram. 4. Below-grade vehicular circulation and total parking area of 27,950 square meters.

East view of the development and waterfront cultural park providing a sculpture garden, amphitheater, culture center, and retail spaces.

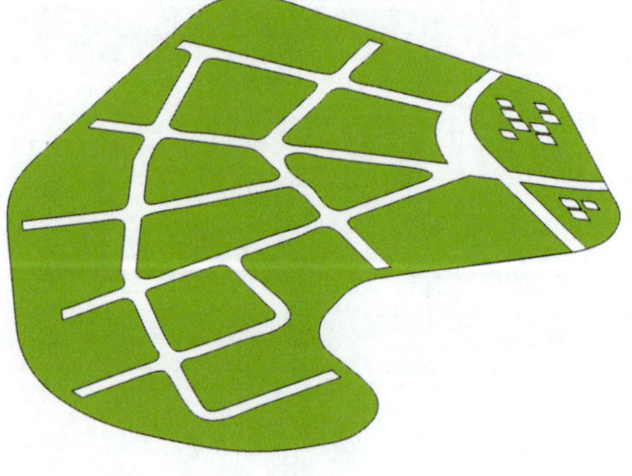

Above: Residential villa island-massing, density, and open-space structure integrate mass and void to create a permeable courtyard residential typology with wide spectrum of private to semi-public open-spaces.

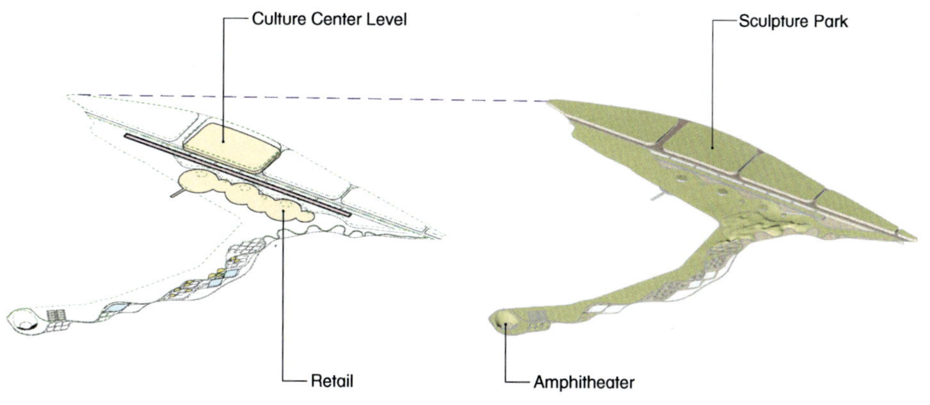

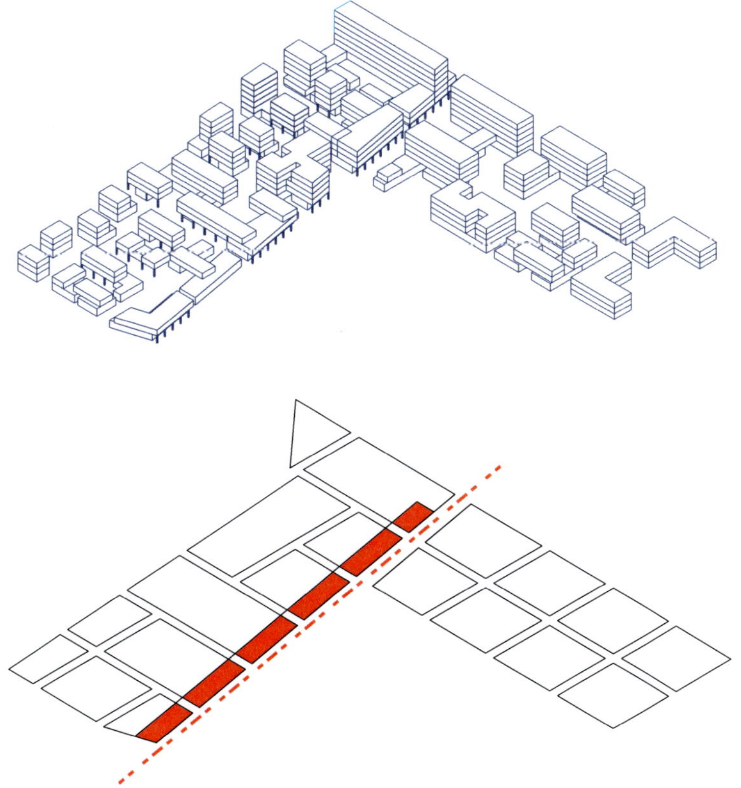

Top: The open space network functions as a recreational park and culture center for the local communities.

Middle and bottom: The central open space functions as the core of the community for the elderly housing island's urban planing and design framework.

Type 1: Hard Edge + Open Space

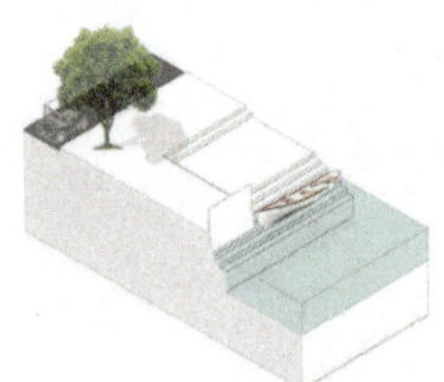

Type 2: Hard Edge + Waterfront Steps

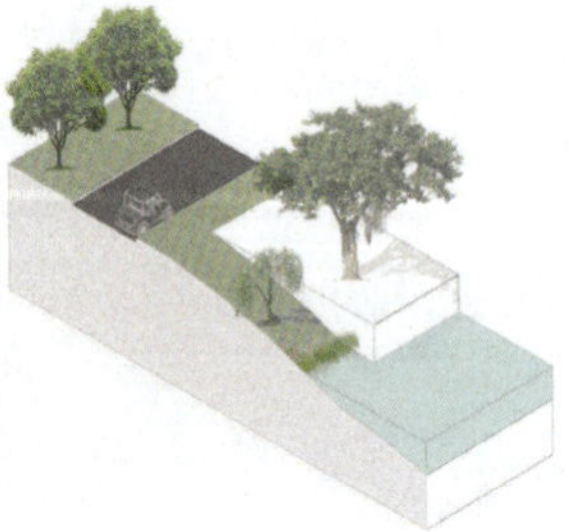

Type 3: Soft Edge + Waterfront Platform

Top: The definitive road structures frame each island's urban and ecological qualities.

Bottom, this and following page: Waterfront edge conditions allow for a spectrum of interaction with the water's ecology.

Following page, top: The villa typology is a reinterpretation of traditional Chinese courtyard houses, assimilating positive mass and negative space to redefine the block perimeter.

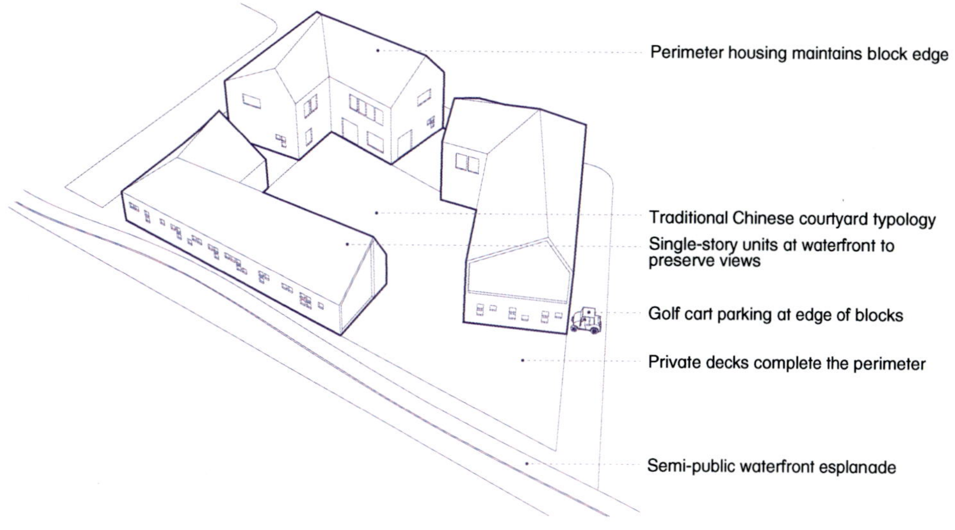

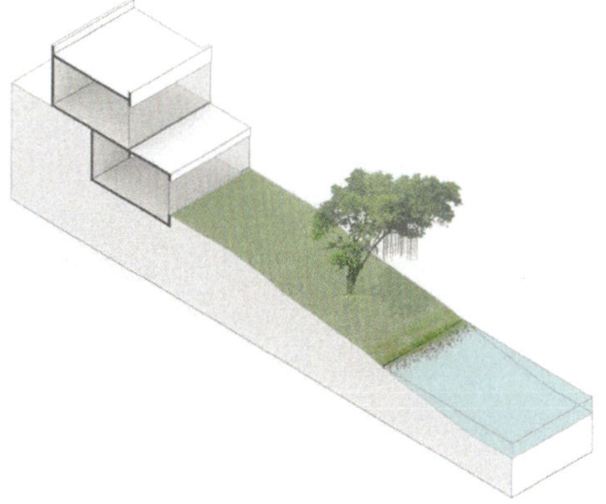

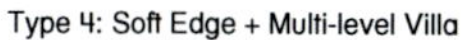
Type 4: Soft Edge + Multi-level Villa

Type 5: Soft Edge + Wood Deck

Project II:

Urbanistic Convergence

Boston, MA USA

Vertical Urbanism: The Pivot

Fabiana Alvear, MAUD
Kyle Trulen, MLA II

We propose a development that reconnects Boston to its waterfront, activates the Rose Fitzgerald Kennedy Greenway, and creates a vibrant atmosphere both day and night, throughout the year. The importance of connecting the city to the water cannot be overstated. Boston is a city of water. Its harbor has been the stage for numerous historical events of local, national, and international significance. Maritime industries propelled Boston to prominence and, as the city grew, it physically extended further into water. In the 1950s, with the construction of the Central Artery expressway, Boston turned its back to the water. Since then the city has spent decades and billions of dollars trying to undo that mistake and the Waterfront has begun to thrive once again.

Boston Harbor, the Greenway, and the New England Aquarium make great, iconic neighbors that draw large crowds, but the Harbor Garage, which occupies one of the last developable sites along the Waterfront, is currently the local eyesore that is dragging its neighbors down. The impenetrable mass of the Harbor Garage blocks views of the water and suffocates the Harbor Walk between the highly active nodes of the Aquarium and Rowes Wharf. Narrow, uninviting sidewalks to the north provide a weak connection between the Greenway and the Aquarium, and the trees of the adjacent plaza block any visual connection between the city and the Aquarium.

“The proposal consists of a diverse mix of uses, encouraging high levels of urban activity both day and night.”

As a new icon for Boston’s skyline, the proposal consists of a diverse mix of uses encouraging high levels of urban activity both day and night. After analyzing market conditions, comparable local developments, and other developments in the pipeline, we determined that a mix of office, hotel, condominiums, retail, and public parking would best achieve these goals. Each side of the proposed development is tailored to address individual challenges and strengthen connections to adjacent neighbors. The project area expands northward, incorporating Central Wharf Plaza, Milk Street, and Central Street, to create strong visual connections from the city to the Aquarium. The development’s west side features a lively mix of retail shops to activate the Greenway while providing visual and physical access from the Greenway to the water’s edge. Terraced seating, waterfront dining, and an urban beach encourage visitors to enjoy the Waterfront. At the intersection of the Harbor Walk and the new public plaza, a water feature connects the seven stories of underground parking with the plaza above. Accessible ramps spiral upward as water falls from above, creating an experience unparalleled along the Waterfront. While transforming a hulking eyesore, this proposed development will forge strong spatial connections with its neighbors by learning from the mistakes of the past to become an integral part of Boston’s future.

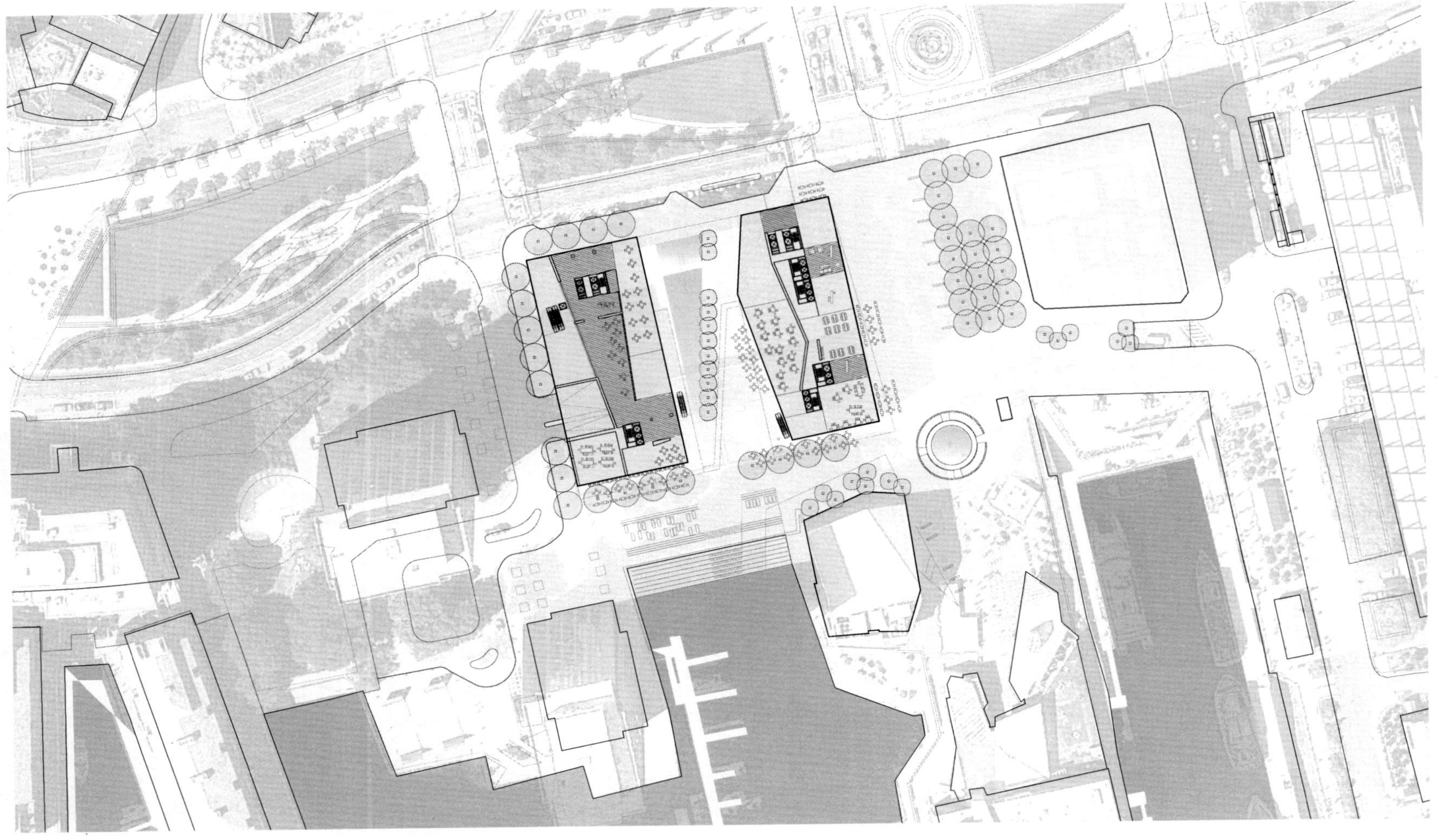

Vertical Urbanism: The Pivot

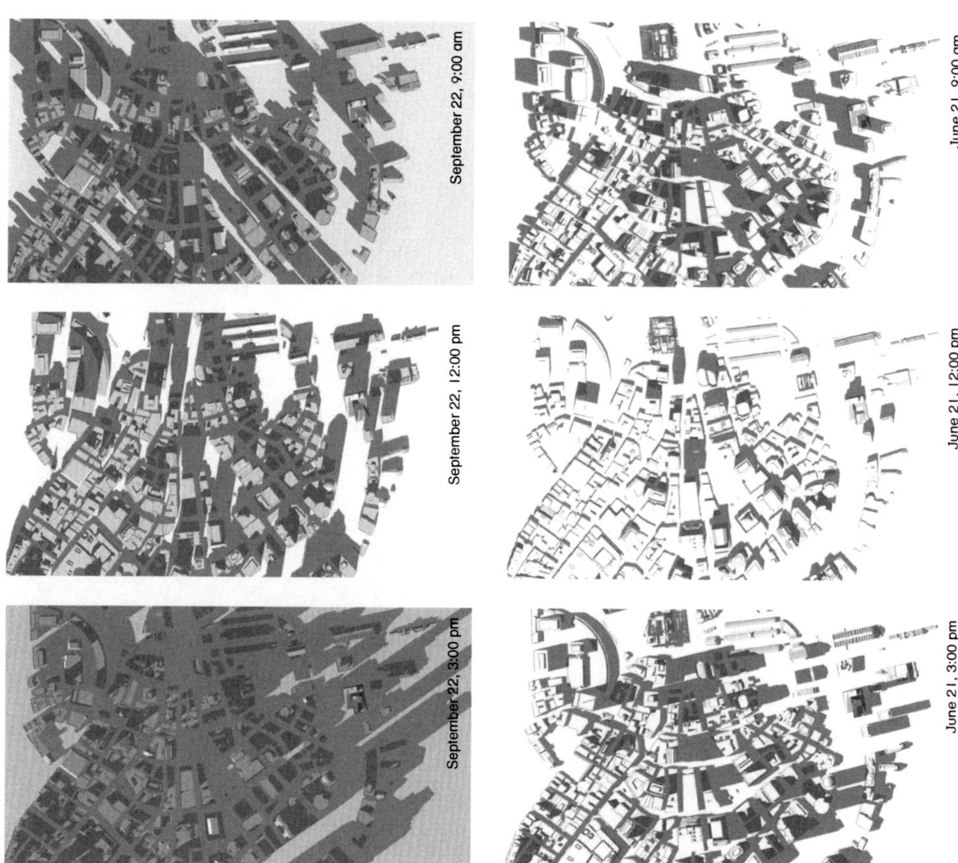

Previous page: Open spaces introduce an active urban connection between the Rose Fitzgerald Kennedy Greenway and the water's edge.

Above: Shadow studies at summer solstice and autumnal equinox inform the sculpting of the high-rise building massing.

Top: The activated Waterfront and the connection to the Harbor Walk create dynamic public open space.

Bottom: The below-grade parking access ramp integrates a light well with a falling water column to embrace the presence of the waterfront and its significance to the project.

Following page: The building massing reflects the contextual urban scale, yet introduces an iconic form to the Boston skyline.

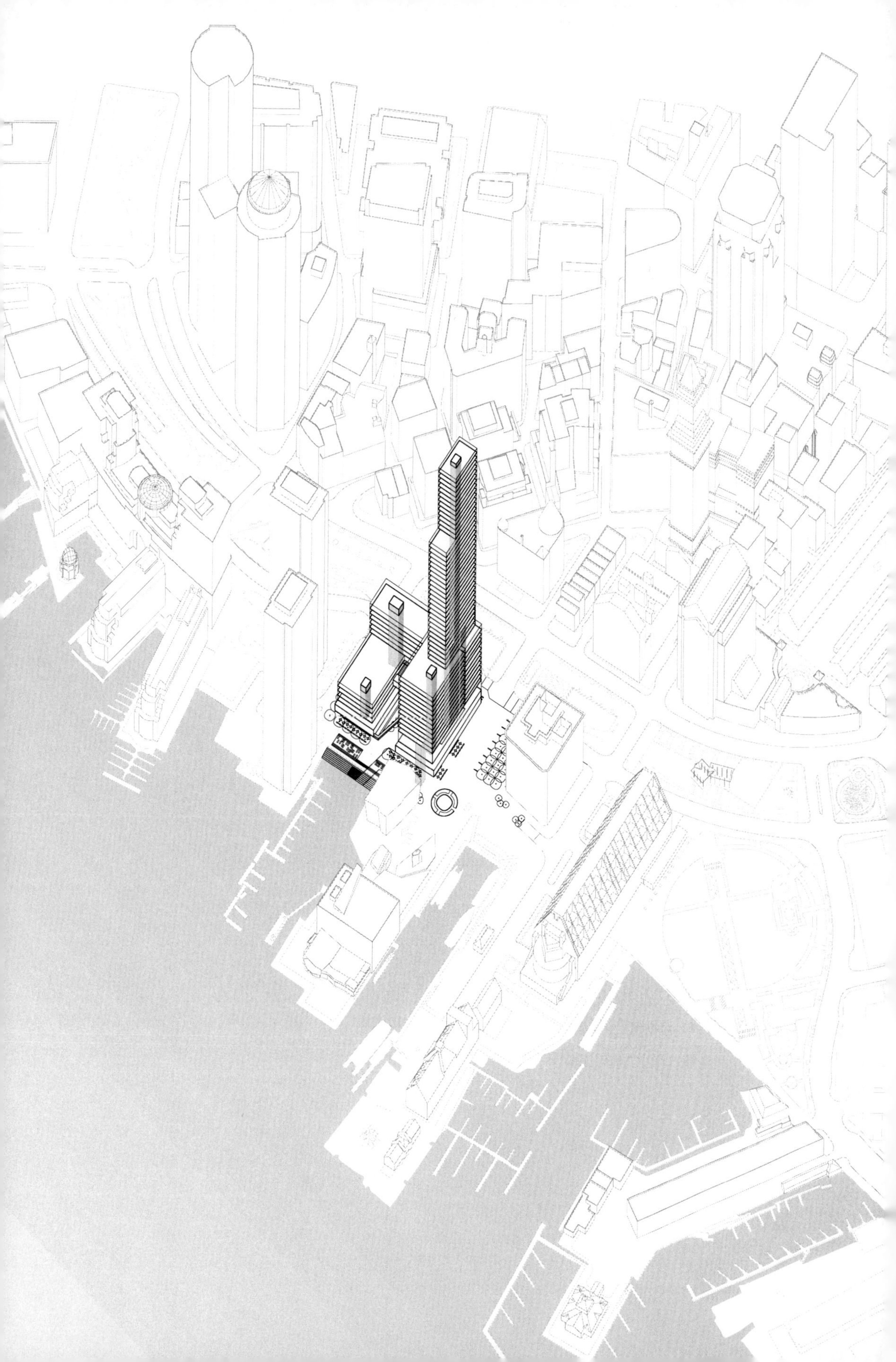

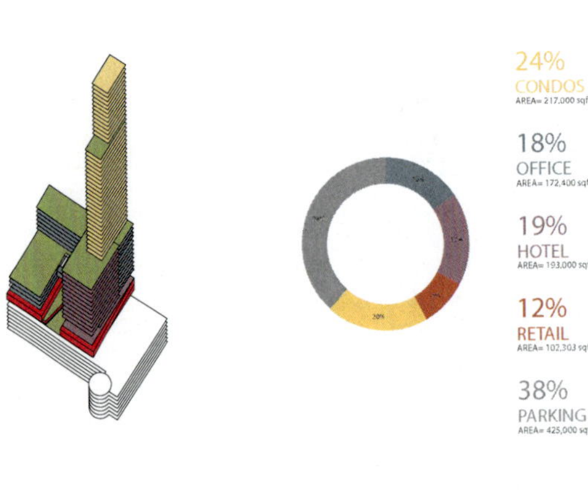

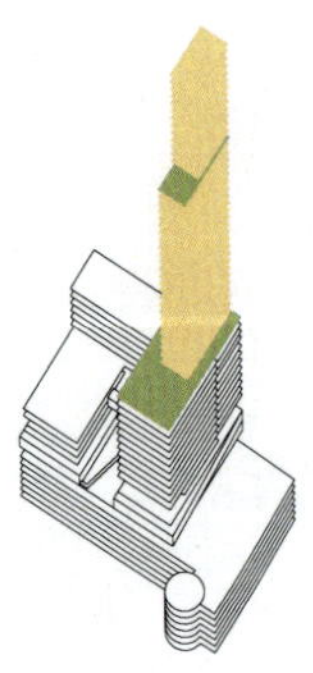

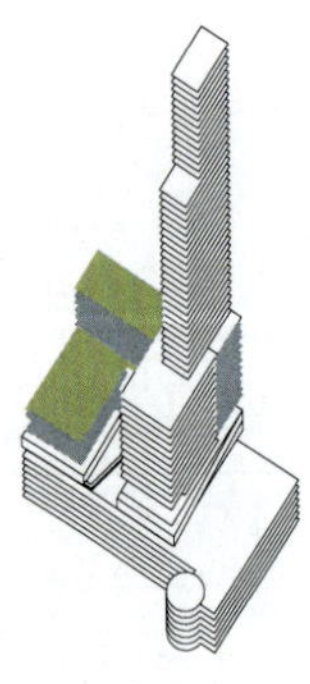

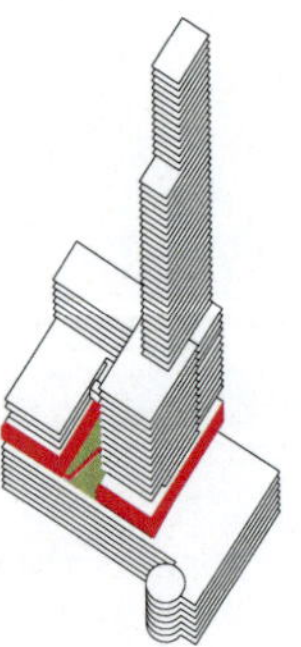

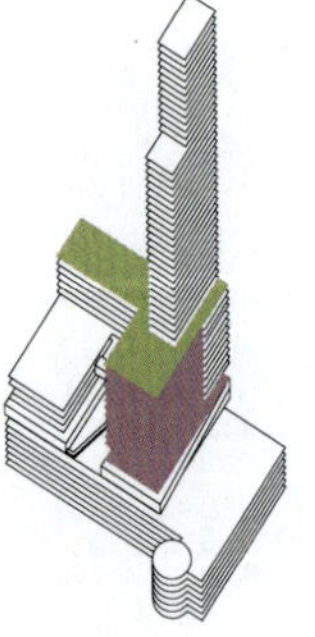

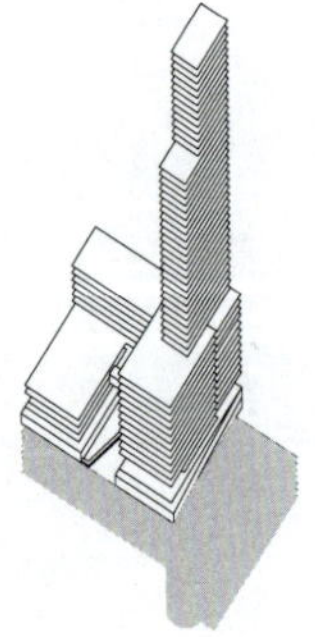

Above: Strategic distribution of programs capitalizes on the site's assets and activates the multilevel public open spaces.

Following page: Sequence of sections defining the dominating presence of the new tower in the Boston skyline.

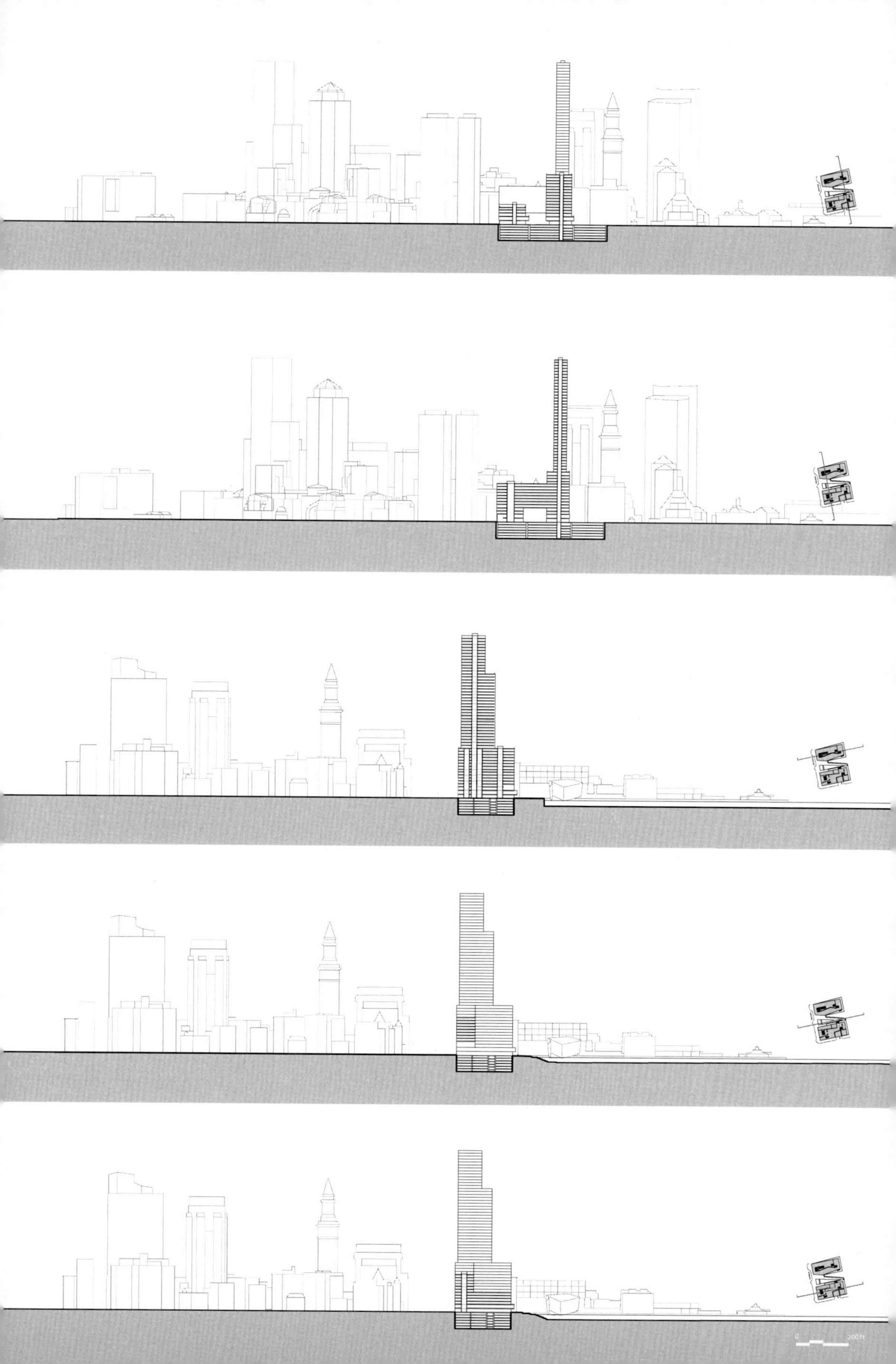
0
200 ft

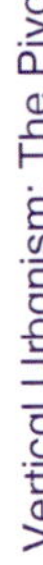

From top to bottom: View from the south, skyline view from the north, waterfront view, a new skyline for Boston.

Following page: Typical plans maximize the floor plate's efficiency and vertical program distribution and adjacency.

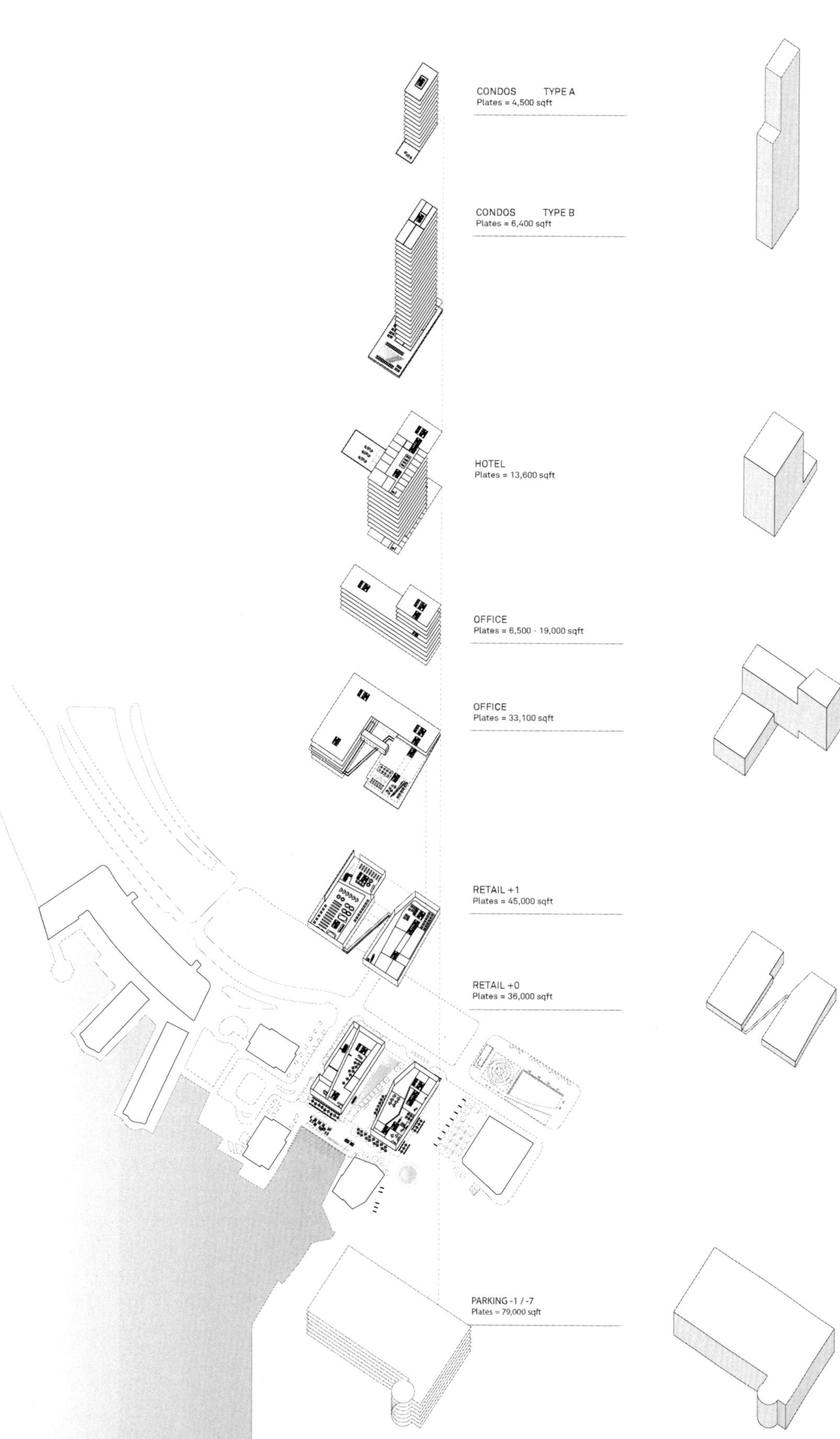
CONDOS TYPE A
Plates = 4,500 sqft
CONDOS TYPE B
Plates = 6,400 sqft
HOTEL
Plates = 13,600 sqft
OFFICE
Plates = 6,500 - 19,000 sqft
OFFICE
Plates = 33,100 sqft
RETAIL +1
Plates = 45,000 sqft
RETAIL +0
Plates = 36,000 sqft
PARKING -1 / -7
Plates = 79,000 sqft

Projecting Context

Thomas Hussey

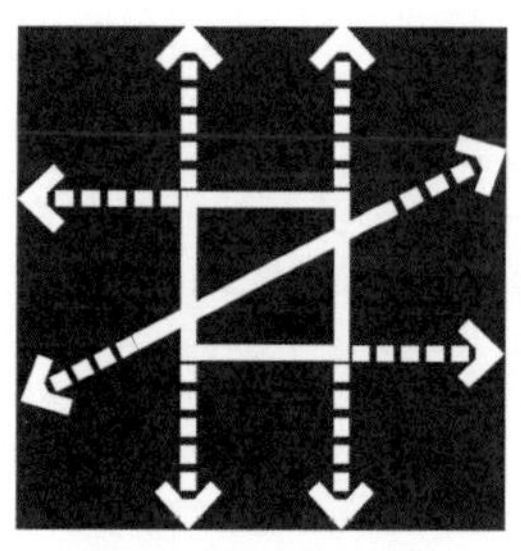

1 INFRASTRUCTURAL CONNECTIVITY

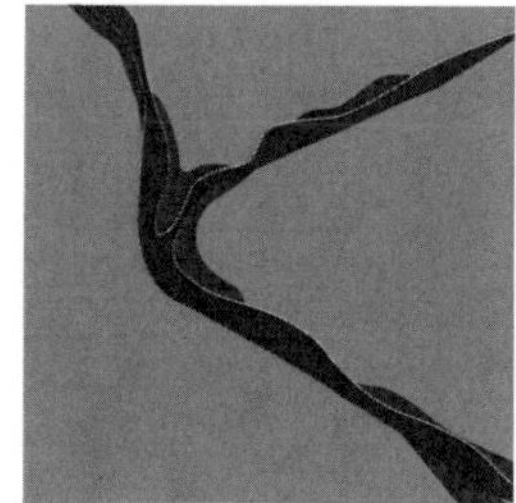

2 ECOLOGICAL HERITAGE

3 LAND-USE LEGACY

4 CLIMATIC CONTEXT

5 TEMPORAL CONTEXT

6 ASPIRATIONS

Six strategies to generate context-based urbanism.

Understanding urban context is of the utmost importance to those engaged in shaping the future of today's cities. Designers of the urban environment study evolutions of the past and current trajectories, ranging from existing physical conditions to environmental impact, from urban heritage to economic outlook, including real estate.

The juxtaposition of two projects in distinctly different geographic and cultural contexts offered the Harvard Graduate School of Design's Spring 2014 Global Leadership in Real Estate and Design course an opportunity to compare and contrast approaches to urban design and development. One project was in the well-established context of downtown Boston, and the other in the dynamic conditions of the expanding periphery of Guangzhou in China.

Boston Harbor Garage Project

A city that has often been mired in its own history, Boston continues to redefine itself. Students addressing the development challenge at the Boston Harbor Garage site discovered a relatively mature urban environment that has benefited from a series of recent improvements. The adjacent Rose Fitzgerald Kennedy Parkway, to name just one catalyst for change, unlocked the development potential of many surrounding parcels of land, prompting developers like the Chiofaro Company, the owner of the subject property, to reconsider the best use for their land holdings.

An abundance of readily available contextual cues can help to facilitate this process, ensuring that subsequent designs are appropriate to place and time, and compatible with the motives of stakeholders. At the same time, such cues can function as powerful constraints that lead to predictable and homogeneous results. The tension between drawing inspiration from context and being limited by it can be seen in the final products of the design teams.

In the case of an established region like Boston, the context is often static in nature and so abundantly obvious, that its translation into a design solution can be handled with swift conviction. There is little need for abstract interpretation or speculation.

Guangzhou Haizhu Lake Project

The Guangzhou project's context presented a striking contrast to that of the Boston site. Located in the alluvial plains of the Pearl River Delta, the area surrounding the Haizhu Lake site is rapidly transforming from an agrarian territory to a densely populated urban district. Despite the fact that a broad-based master plan had been completed for this southern axis district of Guangzhou, much latitude was given to designers, developers, and future government leaders to alter the trajectory of these plans.

The students had had little prior exposure to China's urban environments, and it was evident that they yearned for the contextual cues that typically prompt an approach to design and development. Unlike their counterparts in Boston, who benefited from decades of documentation and solid economic data, these students were largely left to discover, if not to define, the cultural, historical and geographic context in this rapidly developing area. In several cases, if they could not adequately define a context, they invented or projected one to help guide a design concept or development strategy.

For instance, one of the teams (P. Boateng, M. Ciccotti, B. Vargo) sought to reinvent the relationship of the site to water through a series of canals that are typical of other waterfront settlements in the region. Another scheme built upon the typology of an adjacent park and introduced a similar concept on the site—replicating islands of distinct programmatic character (L. Gil, C. Min, H. Wang)—while yet another team (S. Di Leo, A. Locke, T. Lu), inspired by the distant Guangzhou mountains, introduced an artificial mountain on an otherwise flat waterfront site. This diverse collection of projects is a response to the loose contextual cues, but it may also be a product of the whimsical nature of China's development scene, where developers and designers, in an effort to distinguish themselves from the competition and explore new design frontiers, adopt an attitude of "anything goes."

Contextual Strategies

In comparing and critiquing the students' work on the Guangzhou site, several themes became evident. In the absence of any definable physical, economic or social context in this rapidly changing environment, the following strategies often serve as a basis for design and development:

1. Infrastructural Connectivity

The design of new streets, open space, and transit connections becomes an integral part of the existing and future urban fabric. Rather than ignore what might become of the territory surrounding their projects, designers tend to anticipate logical improvements to roads and transit networks, and try to promote contiguous mobility and utility networks as a means of guiding the growth of urban infrastructure in a responsible way.

2. Ecological Heritage
Designers often seek to discover how the land functioned prior to settlement. Ecological heritage is about understanding and reintegrating the ecosystems that are natural to the site, an approach that can result in a more resilient design. This is particularly relevant to the Pearl River Delta: Guangzhou has been consistently ranked as one of the world's most at-risk cities for flood damage due to settlement patterns that have disregarded existing conditions.

3. Land-Use Legacy
When applicable, an exploration of former land uses can lead to the reintroduction of such functions in a contemporary development, or their reinterpretation. For example, urban farming could be integrated on a site that formerly hosted agriculture, or industrial operations in a dense urban fabric, helping to preserve the legacy of the land and maintain the livelihoods of residents who might otherwise be displaced.

4. Climatic Context
A thorough analysis of the local climate is essential in developing a sustainable approach to development. A design should respond to the challenges and opportunities presented by solar, wind, and water conditions. Ideally, this response is manifested in the physical form of the city at multiple scales—buildings, public realm, and district utilities. The goal should be to achieve a high-performance project that is tailored to the specific place and no other.

5. Temporal Context
All cities evolve, and in China and other emerging markets they are evolving rapidly.

Boston's varying urban conditions generated by historical process of urban palimpsest resulting from development and redevelopment cycles.

The recognition that cities will adapt over time is built into any design approach. Creating a flexible framework for growth allows for the redevelopment and adaptive reuse of buildings and infrastructure.

6. Aspirations
In the absence of an established historical context, designers often choose to embrace and promote a lifestyle and culture that will endure long into the future. With many of its cities populated by immigrants and migrant workers, and an economic base that is shifting from agrarian to manufacturing to service, China is striving to establish a position in the global arena. The design of its cities and infrastructure allows a rapid pace of development. In addition to looking backward in time, designers are also thinking about what a city aspires to be in the future.

Projecting Context
In the rapidly developing world, a multifaceted approach is often needed to interpret the urban context, as evidenced by the Guangzhou project. By assembling a series of deeper understandings of where a city has been and where it is going, we can project a context on to a site to serve as the basis for design and development. The point of view could be summarized thus: "In the midst of rapid redevelopment, how do you understand and respect the culture of the place in which you are designing?"

The new generation of designers in China has witnessed two decades of urban development that has left them with a sense of sameness and a yearning for a cultural heritage that is disappearing at an alarming rate. The struggles these locals face are not unlike the challenges the GSD Global Leadership students tackled from afar.

Connection

Thomas Kearns

Recently I had the good fortune to visit the Haystack Mountain School of Crafts in Deer Isle, Maine, designed in 1960 by Edward Larrabee Barnes (Harvard, 1942). Barnes's design is a sublime village connecting land and sea, connecting people to a common purpose of self-discovery and shared discovery.

Human beings have always been drawn to water. Today, nearly half of the world's population lives near a coast (more people than inhabited the planet in 1950, as reported by the United Nations), and the percentage is growing rapidly. Barnes understood, more than 50 years ago, the fragile beauty of the Maine coastline and the potential of Haystack to reframe the sensibilities of future generations of students, faculty, and visitors.

The Global Leadership in Real Estate and Design class syllabus directed teams of students to focus their creativity on two important coastal sites. Like Barnes, the students were confronted by preconceptions and complexities, and charged with reinventing practice paradigms. The best followers make the best leaders. Barnes synthesized his urban planning experiences with his familiarity with the Maine coast. He collaborated with Haystack artists and builders to develop a modernism that was rooted in the regional context. Barnes's goal was "to make things as simple as possible . . . without making them inhuman, dull, or oppressive." This combination of memories, experiences, and collaborations resulted in a development that is profoundly human.

The central stairs function as the axis that connects the waterfront and upland campus at Haystack Mountain School of Crafts.

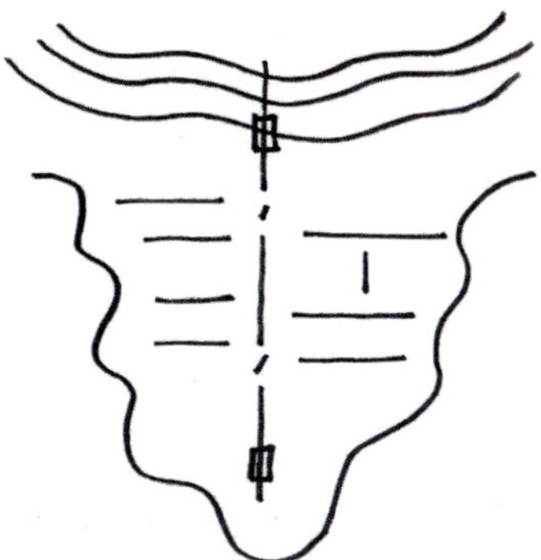

Haystack Mountain School of Crafts is spatially organized to engage the existing topography and the site's natural assets.

Every building contributes to context, influences the environment, and serves communities both present and future. The Guangzhou and Boston development/investment sites have in common a responsibility to connect people to their waterfront. The simple, profound joy of invitation is embedded in each opportunity. Haystack teaches us that every project serves as a lens through which we may reexamine our understanding of our context and our role in the community. As population growth along the coast increases, what if all developments offered a unique portal connecting land to sea, and people to common purpose? The Guangzhou and Boston sites challenge students to conceptualize a global gallery of connectivity, establishing a unique sense of place and contributing to a universal dialog.

Global bodies of water—typically, the intersection of rivers and oceans—have supported human development throughout history. Given the increase in global migration to coastal destinations, with the vast majority of these being long-established waterfront cities, our role as educators and practitioners is to unite diverse stakeholders around a shared set of polemics: privileged vs. underprivileged, exclusive vs. open, short-term vs. long-term, diversity, density, flexibility, identity, competition, etc. Ownership and partnership paradigms can shift considerably when viewed from the water. Waterfront development sites can be seen as a diaphanous tissue encouraging innovation, exploration, and cultural exchange—an organic growth ring.

Above, left: The emerging urban axis of Guangzhou's central business district is aimed at creating a monumental urban axis to connect a series of open spaces from the mainland to the island of Haizhu.

Haizhu Lake Ecological Village, Guangzhou
Harvard GSD design and real estate students are incubating transdisciplinary methodologies to develop proposals for fragile sites. Several teams focused on the Haizhu Lake Ecological Village site in Guangzhou, China. The site is located at the intersection of the Pearl River Delta and the South China Sea. The central problem was organization of the program elements (open space, residential, retail, hotel, and school) combined with vehicular and pedestrian circulation systems within the context of the city and the waterfront. Issues of shared and exclusive use, density, return on investment, and regulatory constraints created a truly complex problem. One team quoted Nicolai Ouroussoff, the former architecture critic of the *New York Times*, who described Guangzhou as "a moribund urban environment."

The student teams understood the essential need for connection. Each team appeared to have developed one conceptual component of an approach to development. One team focused on layers of open space, or "gardens," as a fabric for spatial and communal connectivity. The gardens—botanical, athletic, traditional, sculptural, urban, tea, and courtyard—are skillfully composed. As at Haystack, they form a central spine that appears to connect downtown Guangzhou with the sea. A secondary, nonhierarchical tapestry of open spaces branches off this spine, framing views and creating layers of intimacy and security.

A second team created a well-defined public amenity loop. This vision expanded the site to include adjacent islands that are environmentally sensitive, providing a soft-edge buffer, or eco-corridor, that would help to create a livable community.

A third team focused on a healthy community as the conceptual framework. Three open-space typologies were proposed: mind (people + ideas), body (fitness + recreation), and soul (relaxation + meditation). The programmatic and open-space relationship is clear, with mind (people + ideas) proximate to downtown retail and hospitality, body (fitness + recreation) mid-site and connected to a school program, and soul (relaxation + meditation) at the southern tip of the site. Haystack possesses a similar meditative quality as it gently engages with pedestrians, enticing them to the water, inviting self-reflection.

Each of the student teams connected land to sea and people to water with varying levels of commitment and success. Each struggled to hold on to the clarity of their concept through the design process. While the contexts of downtown Guangzhou and the Pearl River Delta proved challenging, a number of important findings emerged. The development depends on a hierarchy of circulation and

Above, right: Stratified layers of programmed open space and circulation systems structure the Haizhu Gardens development proposal by Patrick Boateng, Matthew Ciccotti, and Brian Vargo.

program from north to south. The potential to reach beyond the site proper and create surrounding zones of influence ensures that this development will not become an isolated community and will provide a healthy environment for people within a healing ecosystem.

Although the solution is specific to Haizhu Lake, it offers guiding principles for other land/water sites around the globe.

Downtown Boston Waterfront

The central problem on the Boston Waterfront was to organize a vision for the program. It has many elements in common with the Guangzhou project, but vertically rather than horizontally. The fundamental question is whether this project typology can be handled with the same care, understated beauty, clarity, and civic grace as Haystack. Can a project with so many requirements, constraints, and masters achieve a state of transcendence and foster self-actualization (Maslow's hierarchy of needs)?

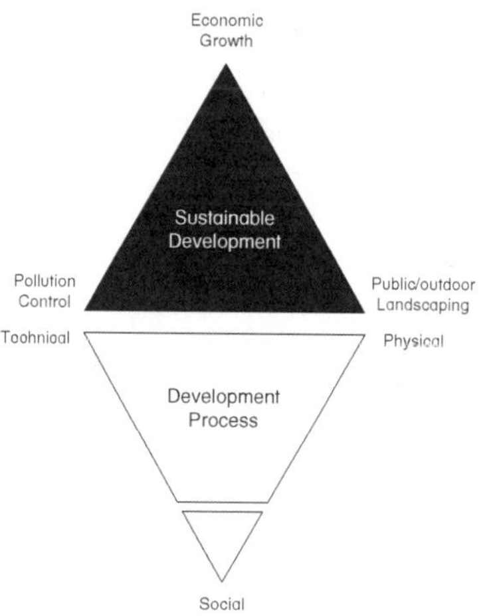

Healthy living and development concept diagram depicting the direct relationship between development process and sustainable development factors.

The problem is one of section. The building will be a "landmark" (definition: "a prominent or conspicuous object on land that serves as a guide, especially to ships at sea or to travelers on a road"). Proposals take on the responsibility of creating a symbolic identity for the city and region as it marks the border between land and water. As at Guangzhou, finding a balance between civic invitation and layering of privatization is the central challenge.

Section also informs the ground-water plane. The various design concepts are easily reinforced by extension into the urban topography of Boston to Tremont Street and Beacon Hill. Sectional analysis has the potential to amplify the energy flow that is inherent in all schemes. As at Haystack, the architecture incorporates a portal inviting descent into Boston Harbor. Conversely, projects that propose access from the water, a connection to Harbor Walk, and ascent to the city center leverage the potential of this site.

While each team's parti is promising, the typical master plan focuses on the development site proper. A multisector methodology would produce a larger district that, in turn, is nested in an urban master plan. Concentric rings of planning reveal the potential for organization of the Harbor Front and the Rose Fitzgerald Kennedy Greenway, and dialog with landmarks such as the Grain Exchange and the Custom House Tower. The New England Aquarium extends into the harbor, while this proposal attempts to bring the harbor to the Greenway. Each solution seeks to expand the range of opportunities and experiences that coastal developments can provide.

Conclusion

The student teams focused on the Guangzhou and Boston sites as prototypical case studies for urban development. They created methodological frameworks for expanding the dialog to multi-sector communities of stakeholders. How to lead, listen, and facilitate are core requirements for the successful development of global waterfront sites, where the stakes are very high. A willingness to seek new questions, take risks, and bring original research to the problem can result in solutions that inspire and, importantly, provide lessons for others.

Monumental Interlace

Chen Ling, MAUD
Emmanuel Torres, MAUD
Heng Zhang, MLA

The Boston Harbor Garage is a significant redevelopment opportunity in the heart of the city's central business district. The design proposal embodies the principles of the Chiofaro Company while grounding the program within the current Boston market as well as in a mixed-use framework. Analysis of the site revealed conflicting shifts in market trends and provided conceptual tension from which the design parti developed.

The proposal is for a single-tower, mixed-used development housing office, retail, residential, and hotel program components that are strategically interlaced in three interconnected towers. The distinct office, residential, and retail programs are vertically deployed to construct synergies among the end users, spatial configuration, and development economics.

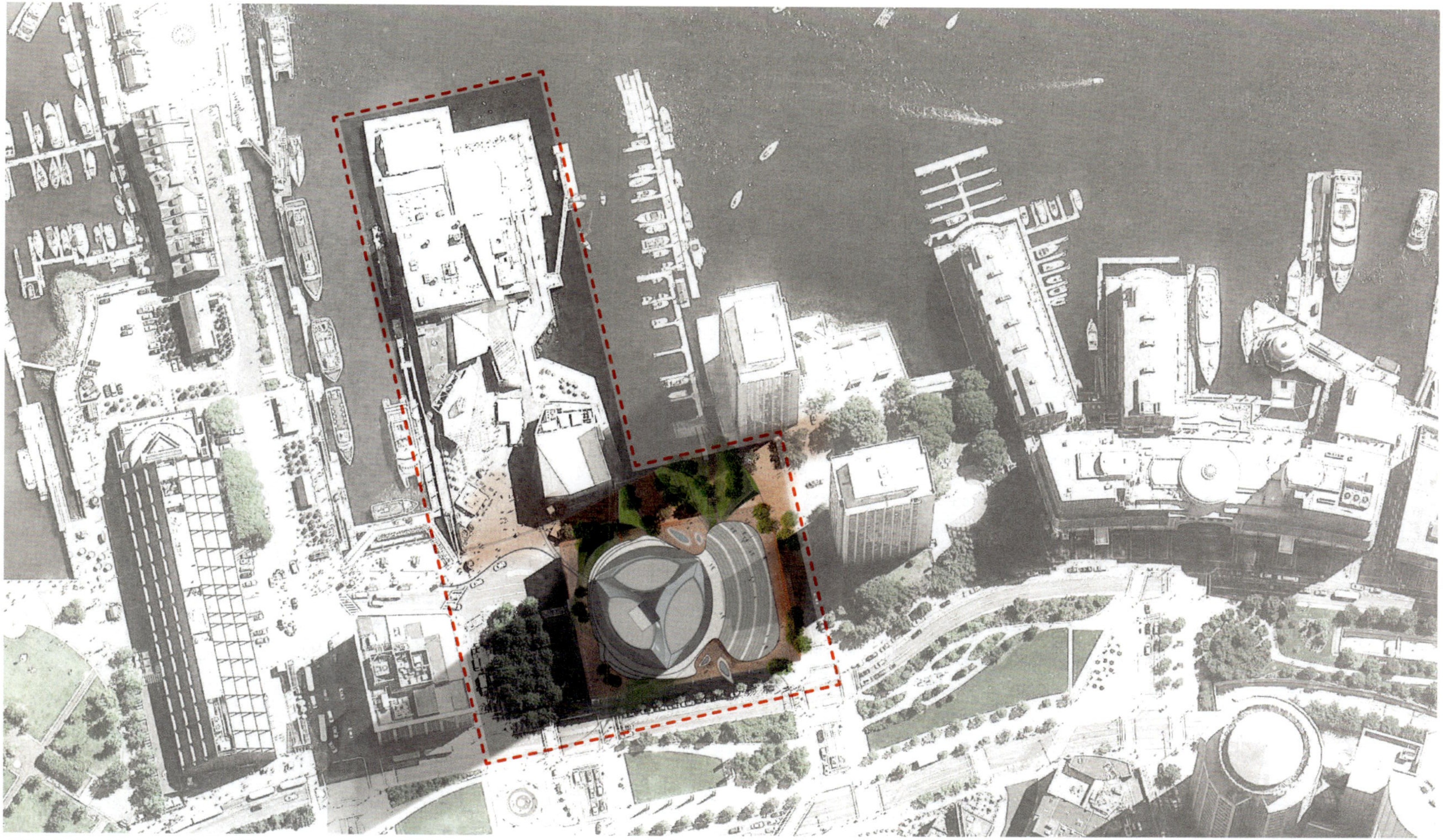

Previous page: A fluid building base promotes active pedestrian access to the Waterfront.

Above: The Harbor Garage site is an important segment to generate a permeable access point to the Harbor Walk and the Waterfront.

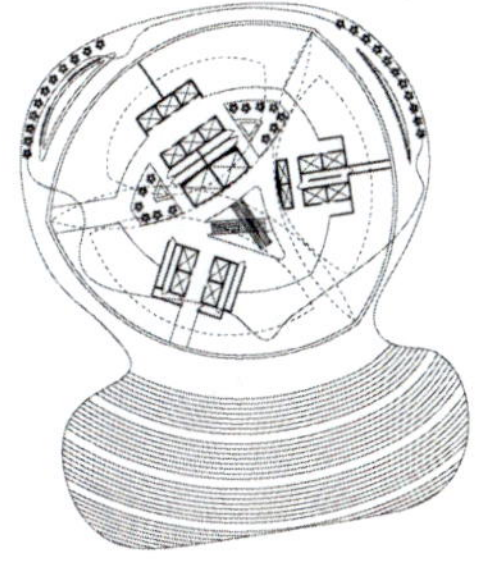

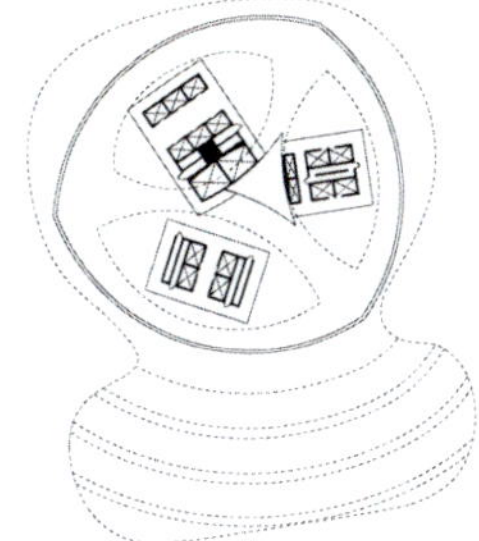

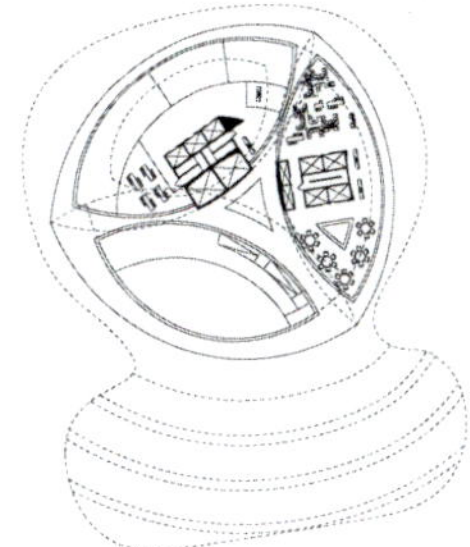

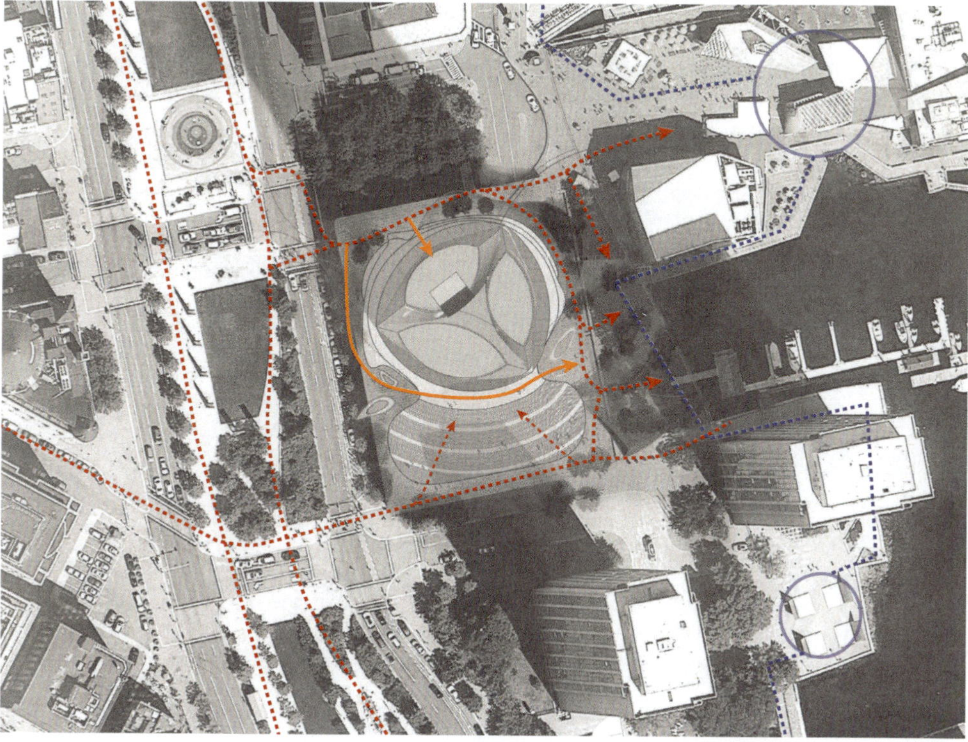

Top: Various program compositions are functionally interlaced within the building massing. From left to right: Retail, Office, Sky Lobby.

Bottom: The site design promotes fluid pedestrian connections from the Greenway to the Harbor Walk, the Aquarium, and the water's edge.

FLOOR AREA RATIO
(FAR)

26.0

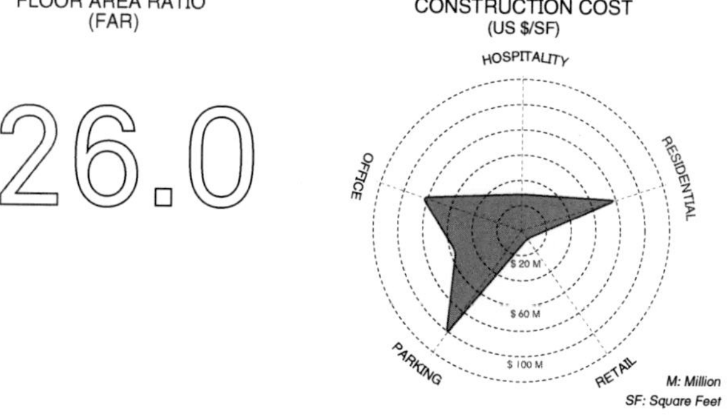

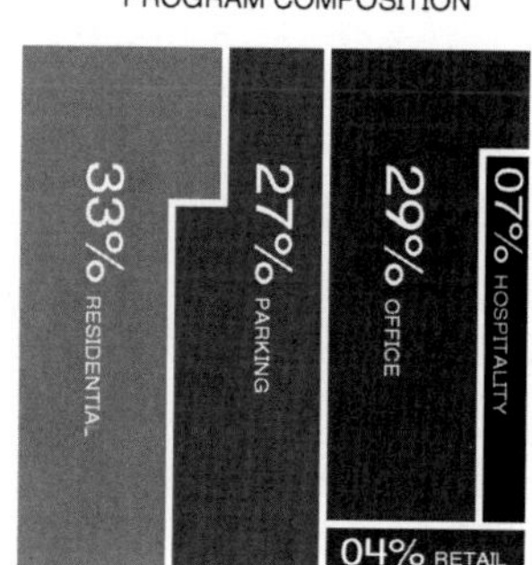

PROGRAM SUMMARY

Program	SF Per Floor	Gross SF	FAR	Cost Per SF (USD/SF)	Construction Cost (USD)
Residential	5,287	556,521	8.5	$ 150.75	$ 83,896,445.25
Parking	65,571	459,000	7.0	$ 225.00	$ 103,275,000.00
Office	15,893	490,066	7.5	$ 175.75	$ 86,129,099.50
Hospitality	5,287	126,880	1.9	$ 225.50	$ 28,611,440.00
Retail	n/a	73,225	1.1	$ 122.50	$ 8,970,062.50
Total Development	n/a	1,705,692	26.0	$ n/a	$ 310,882,047.25

SF: Square Feet
FAR: Floor Area Ratio

Previous page: The tower massing is articulated to respond to the urban context and to optimize the site assets, such as harbor views and solar orientation.

Above: A balanced core program composition with ancillary programs limits exposure to potential risks.

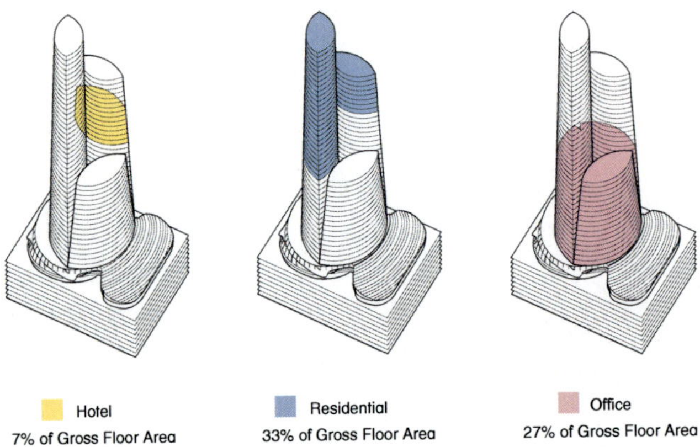

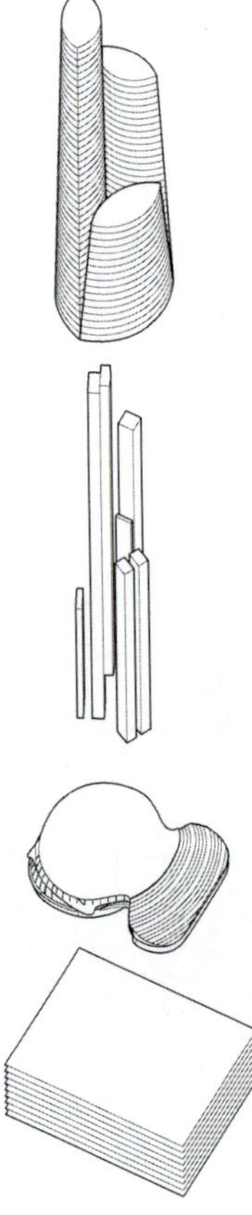

Above: Aggregated towers provide design advantages to construct an efficient interior layout and program allocation.

Following page, top: The terraced tower design allows a hierarchy of leaseable spaces.

Following page, bottom: The permeable retail base provides pedestrian passage to the Harbor Walk and the Waterfront.

Bridging Thresholds: Interconnecting the Boston Waterfront

Alessandro Boccacci, MAUD
Dylan Lazovik, MDes REBE
Ying Zhang, MAUD

The Harbor Garage development process began with an analysis of the urban and market contexts. The Boston Redevelopment Authority (BRA) had articulated an extensive list of objectives, including improved connectivity between the Rose Fitzgerald Kennedy Greenway and the Downtown Waterfront, and the use of gateway moments and art installations to draw pedestrians through the site. While the former mayor's administration had been adamant about dimensional requirements, which would have greatly limited the potential for building on the site, the new administration, in asking, "How tall can you go?", acknowledged that the Waterfront presents an opportunity for a development of considerable height and density.[1]

In a careful examination of the site, the development team identified two centers of activity. To the north, the New England Aquarium (1.3 million visitors a year), the T station, and Quincy Market (18 million visitors a year) form an axis of movement, all with excellent visibility of and proximity to the Harbor Garage. To the south, there was a significant amount of movement between South Station and the Financial District, including International Place just across from the Greenway. The area surrounding the Harbor Garage, however, with its privileged frontages along the Greenway and the Harbor Walk, was notably underutilized, a distinct gap between two vibrant yet disconnected nodes.

Examining real estate trends, the team recognized the exceptional strength of the condominium and hotel markets, particularly the luxury segments. The site's proximity to transit, tourist destinations, and the Financial District made it ideal for hotels catering to leisure and business travelers. The team also saw great potential in using retail as a place-making tool and a means to provide amenities for the surrounding community.

Consideration of specific uses was directly linked to the formal development of the design proposal. With a site of just over 1.3 acres and a goal of satisfying the BRA's mandate for retaining half of this as open space, the team was left to consider how the program would be expressed vertically: one tower or two. As the design progressed, two towers were identified as optimal. The scheme creates a natural break across the site at ground level and includes a retail alley and open space linking the aquarium forecourt and Harbor Walk with the Greenway and the Financial District beyond.

This redevelopment proposal for the Harbor Garage presents a politically viable, financially feasible, and physically beautiful addition to the Boston skyline. The project greatly improves the Downtown Waterfront and creates a vital node to infill the existing spatial and programmatic gap along the Rose Fitzgerald Kennedy Greenway.

1. Paul McMorrow, "How Tall Will a New BRA Go?", *Boston Globe*, April 1, 2014.

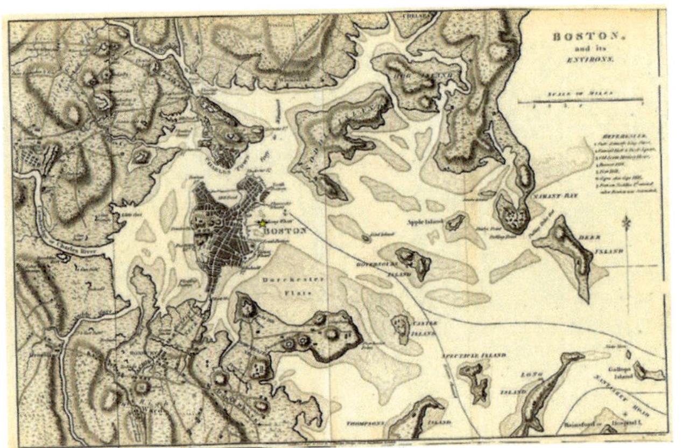

Historical Boston maps describe the expansion of its land area and the length of its waterfront through land reclamation during the city's industrialization and urbanization, periods of intense maritime activity.

Top: 1806 map of Boston. Map reproduction courtesy, the Norman B. Leventhal Map Center at the Boston Public Library. Bottom: 1814 map of Boston. Courtesy, the University of Texas Libraries, The University of Texas at Austin.

Each set of superimposed maps illustrates Boston's transitioning urban and territorial relationships, showing the significance of urban growth and the commercialization of the inner harbor.

Top: 1852 map of Boston. Map reproduction courtesy, the Norman B. Leventhal Map Center at the Boston Public Library. Bottom: 1880 map of Boston by US Census Bureau.

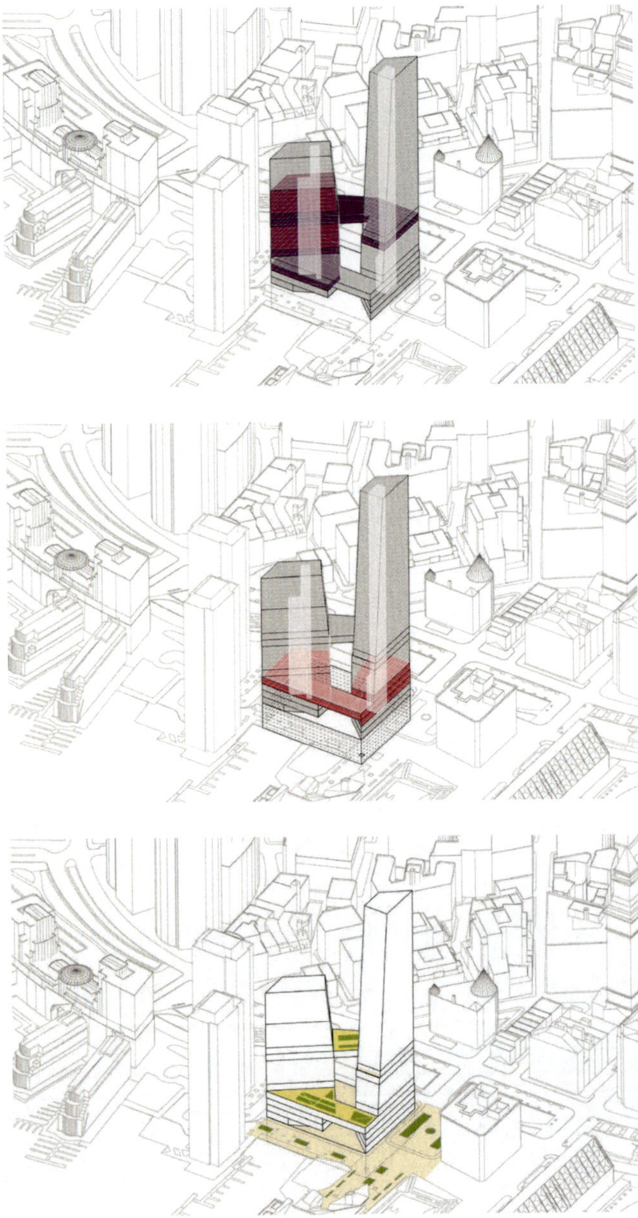

Above: The massing of the two-tower building and the interconnecting programs respond to the existing urban and architectural contexts yet generate iconic spatial experiences.

Following page, top: Luxury condominium sales in Boston are at their highest level since 2007.

Following page, bottom: Boston luxury hotels observed their highest growth in real revenue per available room across all submarkets in 2009.

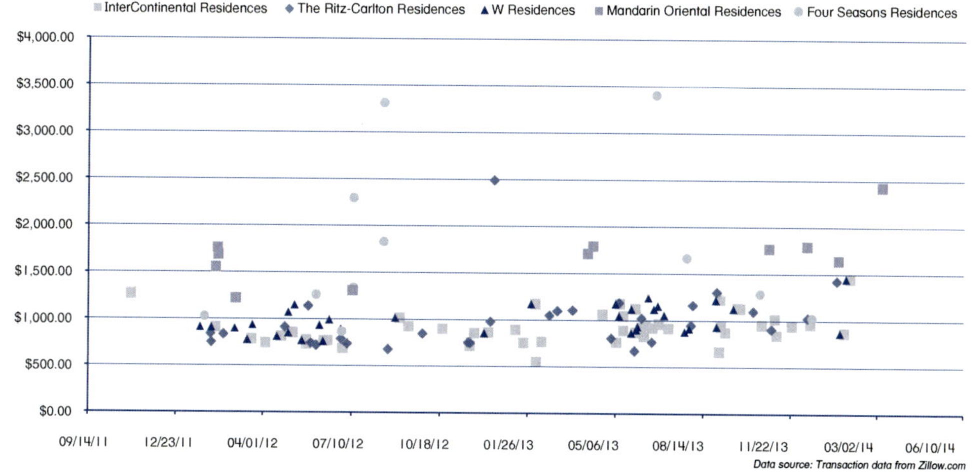

Data source: Transaction data from Zillow.com

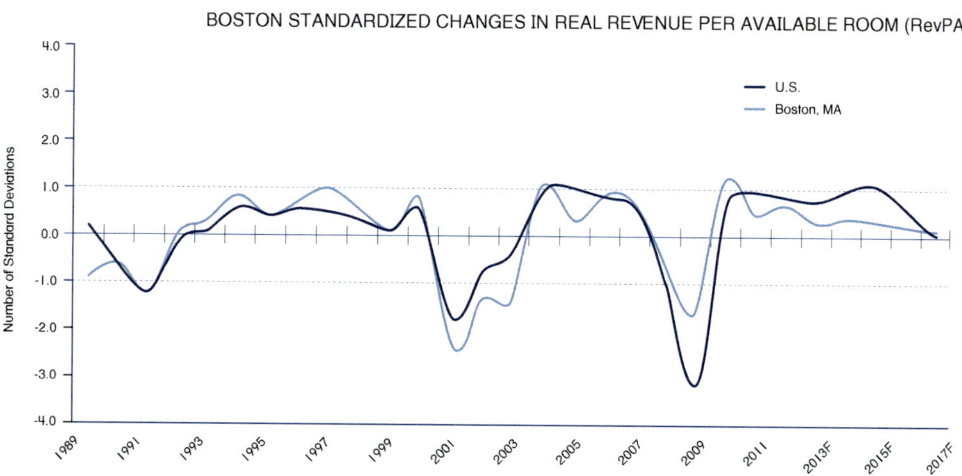

Source: Moody's Analytics, PKF Hospitality Research, LLC, Smith Travel Research

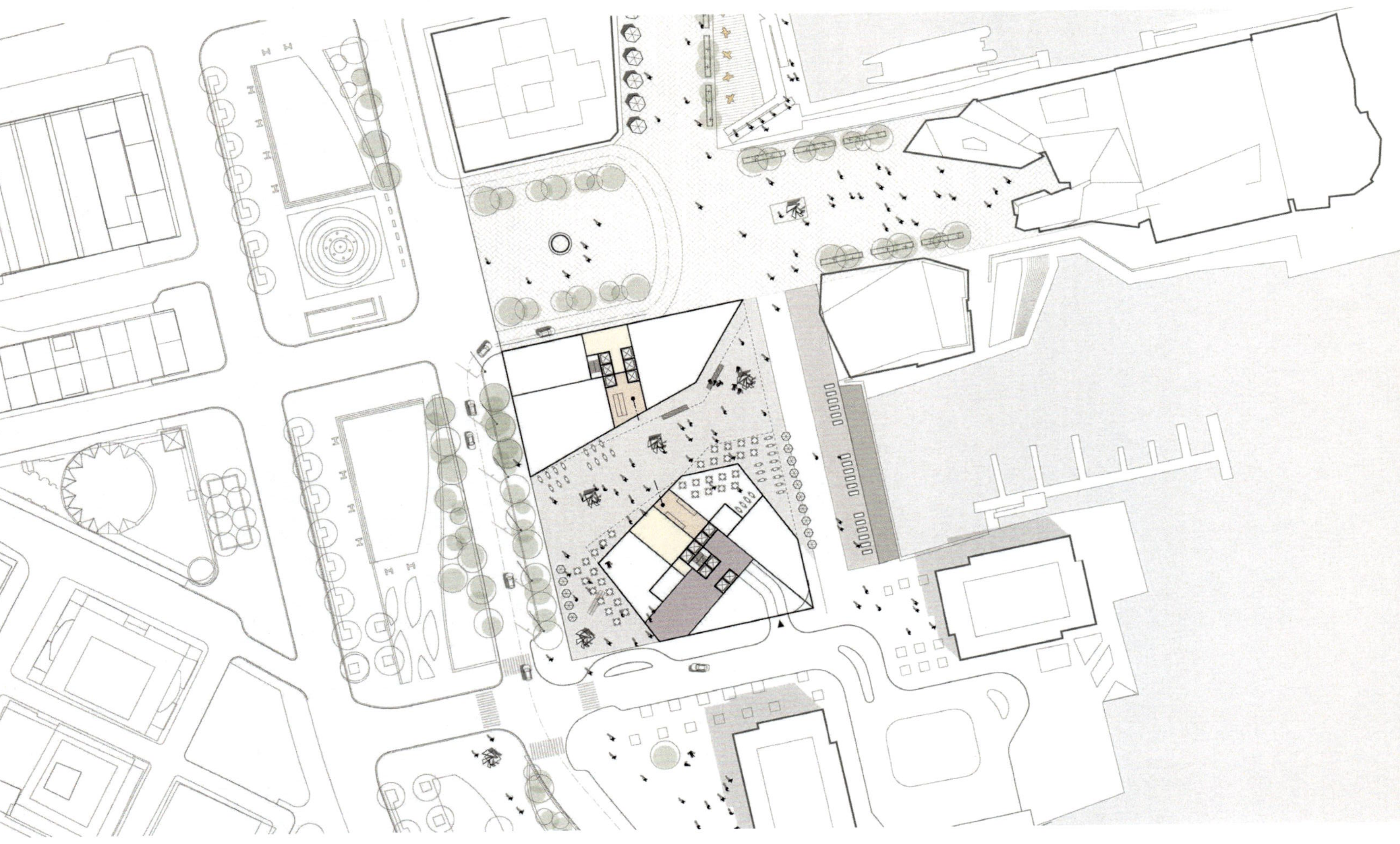

FINANCIAL SUMMARY: CAPITAL STACK, TIMELINE AND RETURNS
TOTAL PROJECT COST: US $703,407,536

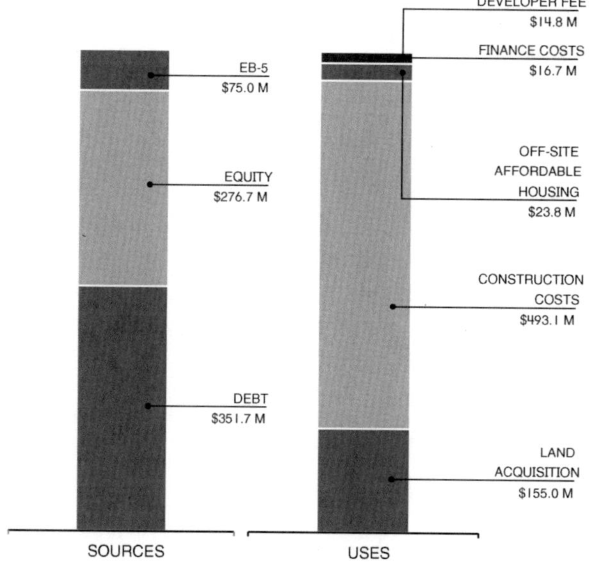

DEVELOPMENT TIMELINE	
Due Diligence	4 months
Permitting	12 months
Construction	24 months
Hold	360 months

EXIT CAP RATE PROJECTIONS	
Hotel	6.75%
Retail	5.00%
Parking	7.75%

PROJECT-LEVEL RETURNS	
Unleveraged IRR	9.3%
Leveraged IRR	19.8%
Leveraged MOC	2.27x

Previous page: The proposed scheme injects new activity nodes to enhance the connectivity of existing centers of activity.

Above: The project will potentially generate an internal rate of return of 19.8 percent with a 360-month hold duration.

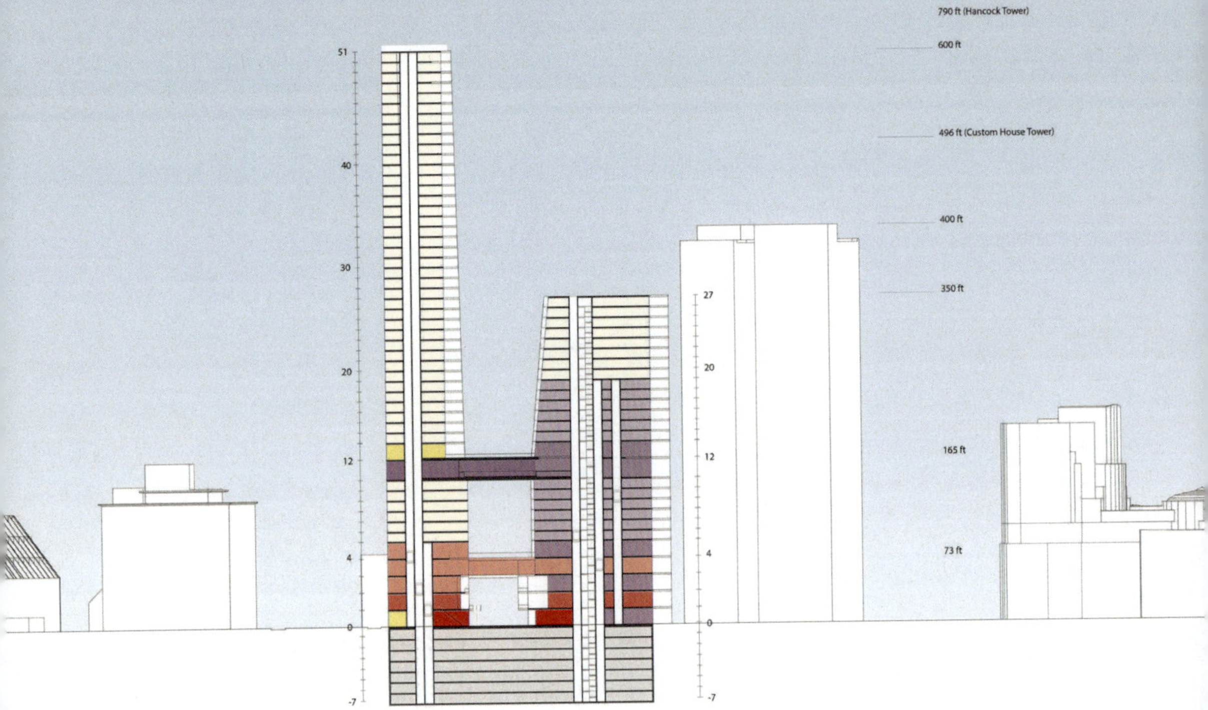

790 ft (Hancock Tower)
600 ft
496 ft (Custom House Tower)
400 ft
350 ft
165 ft
73 ft
51
40
30
20
12
4
0
-7
27
20
12
4
0
-7

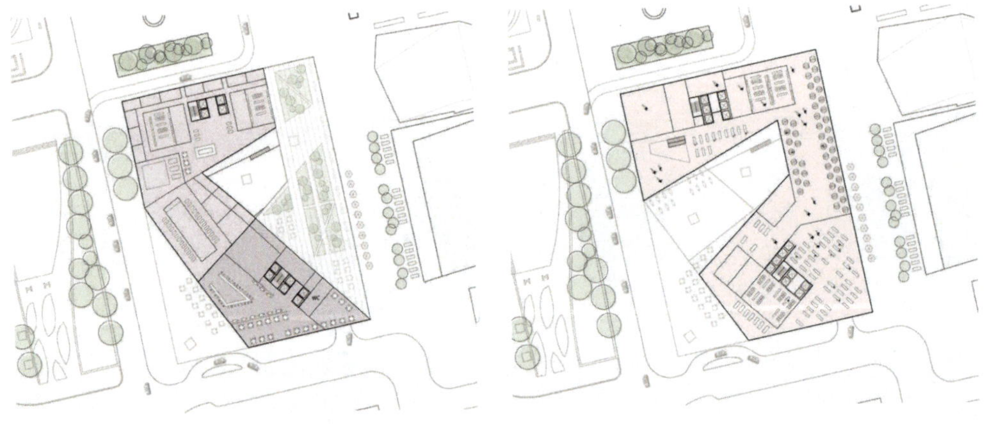

Top: Program stack diagram of the secondary massing tower looking south.

Bottom: Public program bridges link the two towers at multiple levels.

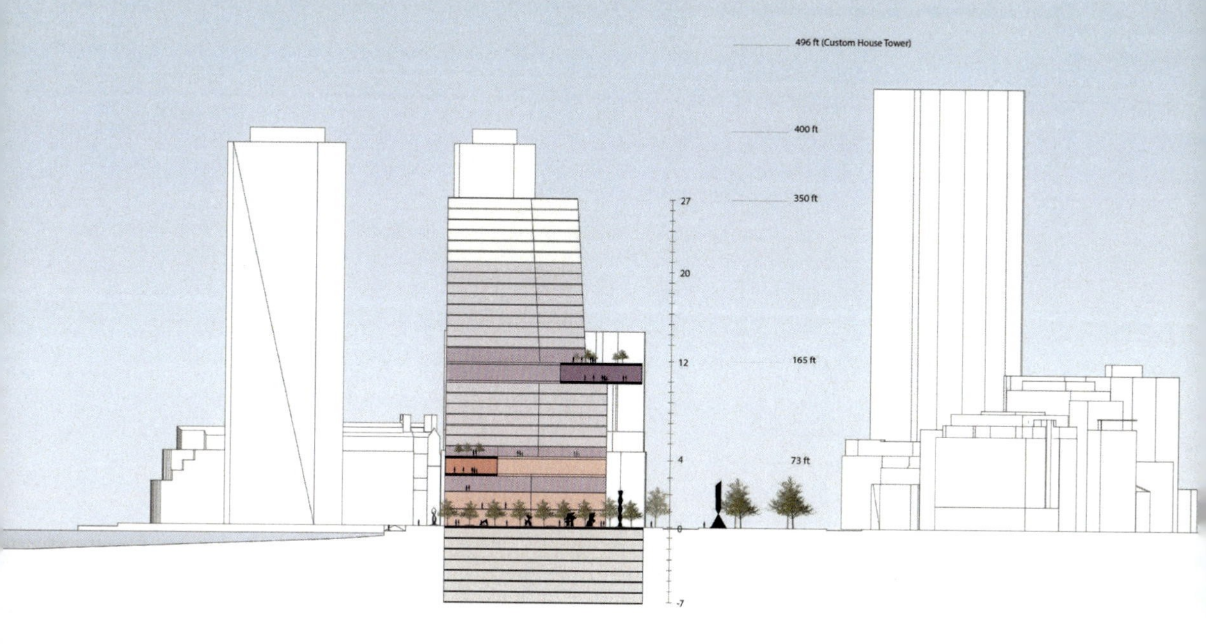

Top: Stack diagram looking east shows integration of uses and relationship to surrounding structures.

Bottom: Opening up the block and creating a retail arcade enhances pedestrian flow and conductivity between the Greenway and Harbor Walk.

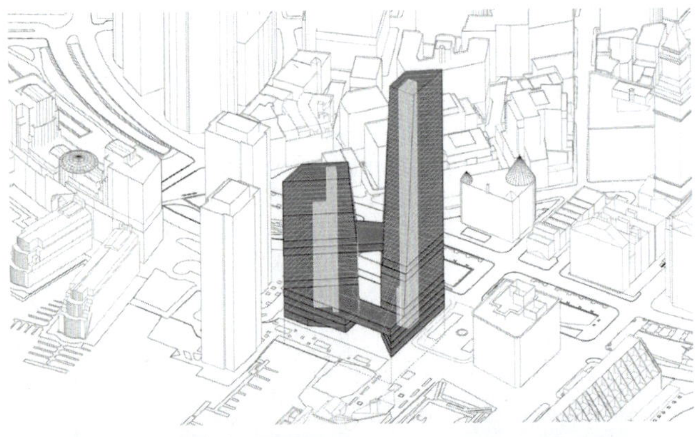

Above: The permeable public plaza interconnects the Greenway and the harbor waterfront visually, physically, and programmatically.

Following page: The placement of the two tower massing was carefully considered to maintain view corridors between existing buildings and city icons.

The massing blends with the existing skyline, while adding a tall, slender beacon that references the Custom House Tower in profile.

Bing Wang
DDes, is Associate Professor in Practice of Real Estate and the Built Environment at the Harvard University Graduate School of Design (GSD). She is also a faculty co-chair for the GSD Advanced Management Development Program, and a faculty co-chair for the joint GSD and Harvard Business School (HBS) Real Estate Management program. Dr. Wang leads a design practice, HyperBina Design Group, and a real estate company, YongYou Investments, in the United States and China. Her publications include *The Architectural Profession of Modern China: Emerging from the Past* (2011), *Prestige Retail* (2014), and *Understanding Real Estate Investments in China* (forthcoming), among others.

A. Eugene Kohn
FAIA, RIBA, JIA, as a co-founder and principal of Kohn Pedersen Fox Associates, has led the firm to become one of the world's most respected and innovative architectural design practices. Known for his inspirational leadership and commitment to design excellence, Kohn is a skillful collaborator who brings together diverse project teams to create buildings that contribute to their surroundings on both functional and social levels.

Sven Andersen
is a Partner of KPMG Germany, Co-Head of Corporate Finance Real Estate Germany, and Head of Real Estate M&A, located in Germany. He concentrates on real estate mergers and acquisitions, debt advisory, and loan sales. Prior to joining KPMG in January 2009, Andersen headed the Real Estate Investment Banking Division for Germany, Austria, and Switzerland at Lehman Brothers. From 1997 to 2006 he worked for Deutsche Bank, inter alia in the corporate development department. He holds a Master's Degree of Science in Economics.

Thomas Hussey
AIA, LEED AP, is a Director of Urban Design and Planning in the Chicago office of Skidmore, Owings and Merrill. As an architect and urban designer, he leads multidisciplinary design teams to creatively address the challenges and opportunities emerging from established and developing cities worldwide.

Blair Kamin
has been architecture critic of the *Chicago Tribune* since 1992. A graduate of Amherst College and the Yale School of Architecture, he has been a fellow at the Neiman Foundation for Journalism at Harvard University. The University of Chicago Press has published two collections of Kamin's columns: *Why Architecture Matters: Lessons from Chicago* (2001) and *Terror and Wonder: Architecture in a Tumultuous Age* (2010). Kamin is the recipient of 35 awards, including the Pulitzer Prize for Criticism, which he received in 1999 for a body of work that included a series of articles about the problems and promise of Chicago's lakefront, its greatest public space.

Thomas D. Kearns
AIA, LEED AP, is President of DSK | Dewing Schmid Kearns Architects + Planners, located in Concord and South Dartmouth, MA. His practice focuses on planning and design for institutions including Harvard, Boston Children's Hospital, MIT, Duke, Johns Hopkins, and Rhode Island School of Design. At Harvard's Graduate School of Design, Kearns co-leads two programs, Leading Organizations, and the Advanced Management and Development Program Team Project.

Yong K. Kim
is an Urban Designer and Design Associate at HyperBina Design Group, focusing on development strategies and resilient design projects for urban environments. Kim's urban design projects have been internationally recognized through publications and awards including the AIA and ASLA National Honor Awards. Kim received his MAUD degree from Harvard University Graduate School of Design and his BFA and BArch degrees from Rhode Island School of Design.

Thomas Schneider
D.Ec., is cofounder and co-CEO of the online real estate investment platform Brickvest. In his role, he is responsible for developing strategic partnerships, deal underwriting, and setting the long-term strategy for the company. Schneider previously held positions at leading financial institutions such as Lehman Brothers, KPMG, and Ernst & Young, focusing on real estate investment banking and corporate finance advisory. Schneider received his undergraduate degree in Business Administration and Doctor of Economics from the University of Erlangen-Nuremberg, an MSc in Real Estate Development from Columbia University, and an MDes in Real Estate from Harvard University.

Colophon

Global Leadership in
Real Estate and Design
Instructors
Bing Wang, A. Eugene Kohn
Report Editor
Bing Wang
Report Design
Yong K. Kim, HyperBina Design

A Harvard University Graduate
School of Design Publication
Dean and Alexander and Victoria Wiley Professor of Design
Mohsen Mostafavi
Assistant Dean for Communications
Benjamin Prosky
Editor in Chief
Jennifer Sigler
Senior Editor
Melissa Vaughn
Associate Editor
Leah Whitman-Salkin
Publications Coordinator
Meghan Sandberg
Copyediting
Mary Crettier

Series design by Laura Grey and Zak Jensen

ISBN 978-1-934510-49-0

Acknowledgments
Mohsen Mostafavi, K. Michael Hays, Pat Roberts, Rahul Mehrotra, Peter G. Rowe

Image Credits
Cover: © HyperBina Design
Page 19: Map source: Guangzhou Urban Planning Bureau
Pages 34–35: Matthew Ciccotti
Page 39, top: Christine Min
Page 39, bottom: Aaron Locke
Page 50: Map by D. Vrooman
Pages 78–79: HelloGreenway
Page 91: Courtesy Thomas Hussey
Page 93: Emmanuel Torres
Page 95, image and diagram: Thomas Kearns
Page 96, left: Frankie Refuerzo
Page 97: Zhewen Dai, Jason McAlees, and Frankie Refuerzo

The editors have attempted to acknowledge all sources of images used and apologize for any errors or omissions.

Harvard University
Graduate School of Design
48 Quincy Street
Cambridge, MA 02138

publications@gsd.harvard.edu
gsd.harvard.edu

Made in the USA
Middletown, DE
26 February 2019